THE VISUAL FACTORY

Building Participation
Through Shared Information

THE VISUAL FACTORY

**Building Participation
Through Shared Information**

Michel Greif

Foreword by
Bruce Hamilton
United Electric Controls Company

Publisher's Message
Norman Bodek
Productivity, Inc.

Productivity Press, Inc.
Cambridge, Massachusetts   Norwalk, Connecticut

Originally published as *L'Usine S'Affiche*, copyright © 1989
by Les Editions d'Organisation.

English translation copyright © 1991 by Productivity Press, Inc.
Translated by Larry Lockwood.

Productivity Press, Inc.
P.O. Box 3007
Cambridge, MA 02140
(617) 497-5146

Cover design by Joyce C. Weston
Typeset by Rudra Press, Cambridge, MA
Printed and bound by Arcata Graphics Halliday
Printed in the United States of America

Library of Congress Cataloging-in-Publication Data

Greif, Michel.
 The visual factory : building participation through shared information /
Michel Greif.
     p.   cm.
 Translation of: L'usine s'affiche.
 Includes bibliographical references and index.
 ISBN 0-915299-67-4
 1. Communication in management.   2. Communication in organizations.
3. Visual communication.   I. Title.
HD30.3.G7413   1991   90-48170
658.4'5 — dc20   CIP

91   92   93   10   9   8   7   6   5   4   3   2   1

Contents

Acknowledgments

This book would not have been written without my being allowed to observe certain plants, where nothing was concealed. The hospitality and assistance that I received enabled me to obtain the necessary information. Thus, I wish to express my fullest appreciation to all of their personnel – workers, administrative staff, executives, and management.

Bendix Electronics, Toulouse, France; Bull, Angers, France; Case Tenneco, Washau, Wisconsin; Citroën, Caen, France; Digital Equipment Corporation, Colorado Springs, Colorado; Ernault Toyota, Cholet, France; Facom, Nevers, France; Favi, Hallencourt, France; Fichet Bauche, Oustmarest, France; France Abonnements, Chantilly France; Fleury Michon, Pozauges, France; Gorman Rupp, Ohio; Hewlett-Packard, Cupertino, California; Hewlett-Packard, Fort Collins and Greeley, Colorado; Hewlett-Packard, Grenoble, France; Hewlett-Packard, Sunnyvale, California; NUMMI, Fremont, California; Omark, Oroville, California; Physio Control, Seattle, Washington; Poclain, Carvin, France; Renault, Sandouville, France; J. Reydel, Gondecourt, France; Société Anonyme de Télécommunications, Lannion, France; Simpson, Shelton, Washington; Solex, Evreux, France; Télémécanique, Carros, France; Valeo, La-Suze-sur-Sarthe, France.

I also wish to express my thanks to Berco Grimbert, who introduced me to the world of manufacturing when I was a young engineer, and who taught me to appreciate properly performed work.

I must likewise express my gratitude to the entire teaching staff at the Hautes Etudes Commerciales campus at Jouy-en-Josas, and more specifically to professors Gérard Baglin, Olivier Bruel, Alain Garreau, and Lucien Maeder, because my contact with them enabled me to broaden my view of industrial management. The experts at the Centre International de la Pédagogie d'Entreprise (CIPE) also provided valuable advice and opened many doors for me. Hence, I hope that Christian Moisy and Eric Pesnel are aware of my gratitude.

Lastly, it is impossible for me to forget the extent to which my wife, Rosa Laura Fischbein Greif, was responsible for this book. She deserves recognition, both for her expertise in the fields of psychology and communication, which provided valuable insight in regard to my topic, and for constantly placing the bar slightly higher, enabling me to exceed my expectations.

Michel Greif

Foreword

The traditional workplace is filled with visual cues. Its rows of fluorescent lamps, tiled floors, and maze of benches and shelving describe a place in which labor resides. Communications *to* labor are posted on bulletin boards: yellowing legal announcements, vacation schedules and labor rates, a poster exhorting workers to observe safety regulations. Next to the bulletin boards are locked suggestion boxes, representing labor's voice to management.

Even today, this scene is repeated in many factories that I visit. The factory, as Michel Greif notes, speaks to us, and too often its conveyance is one of mutual distrust, one-way communication, and lack of regard for the intellectual potency to be found on the factory floor.

How can we change? In *The Visual Factory*, Michel Greif has collected dozens of specific examples of successful and unsuccessful uses of visual techniques juxtaposed in such a way as to indicate what has to be done and *un*done to create the visual factory. These cases all demonstrate that visual control is not just a technique to be layered onto traditional contexts for communication. It is a new medium for communication that can work only in a new context.

As a medium, visual communication is "a message in search of an author." Unlike traditional announcements, the visual message is not directed to a specific party. It is more like an advertisement to which any employee may be drawn; each person who subscribes to the message becomes, in a sense, its author. The visual factory is one in which communication is in the eye of the beholder. Techniques such as *kanban, jidohka, andon,* and CEDAC* all draw the factory's *public* to the message rather than pushing data under the noses of a select few supervisors or managers. Information, which for many decades has been decoupled from production, becomes re-integrated in a form that adds meaning to each production task.

The medium defines a new context, one in which departmental and hierarchical boundaries are expanded. Sharing of information is sharing of power and control. Transforming the traditional atmosphere of mutual distrust to one more favorable to visual communication is a far greater challenge than educating for and practicing particular techniques. Achieving a visual factory requires first that we achieve a *visible* factory: one that respects and encourages the wisdom and experience of all employees, one in which continual discourse between departments is occurring, and one in which management walkabouts are commonplace. Specific cases named in *The Visual Factory* are especially useful for companies who are ready for an all-out attack on the status quo but aren't sure how to begin.

The power of visual cues is before us every day, yet for lack of our awareness it goes largely unrecognized. At United Electric, we discovered only after several years of continuous improvement efforts that public sharing of information within the factory is inseparable from public motivation for improvement. This translation of Michel Greif's *Visual Factory* provides a fresh "visual perspective" of techniques for continuous improvement, placing them into the real space of real factories.

Bruce Hamilton
Vice President of Manufacturing
United Electric Controls Company
Watertown, Massachusetts

---

* CEDAC is the registered service mark of Productivity, Inc.

Publisher's Message

Can you imagine playing in a baseball game where no one knows the score? Your team is scoring, the other side is also hitting, and a few bogus calls from the umpire may grab your attention for a little while. But how long will you maintain real interest in the game? A score makes the action interesting by defining what it means to win and whether the team has a chance to win. It tells players how the team is doing and how their individual efforts contribute to its success – in short, what they need to do to win.

The situation is not so different for the players in the game of industry: the men and women who work in factories. *The Visual Factory* is a book with a message that is long overdue: Employees are intelligent individuals who are motivated by work that keeps them informed about how their efforts affect the outcome and gives them the power and responsibility to reach their goals.

For many years, companies operated under precisely the opposite assumption. On the production floor and in the office, management assumed the ignorance of workers, divided the work into simple, repetitive tasks, and controlled people's efforts through authoritarianism and confrontation. Information sharing was not an issue: All information was in the hands of the bosses, and workers were kept in the dark.

The factory game today is changing. It has to. Modern manufacturing management strategies cannot be adopted successfully in an authoritarian organization. They require a partnership among workers, managers, and skilled and technical staff in which the parties are responsible to each other for the outcome. And to produce that desired outcome, all partners must be informed and working together.

Visual communication is self-service information — it makes the same information commonly available and understandable at a glance to all who view it. This sharing of information brings a new light and life to the culture of the workplace. *The Visual Factory* shows some of the major ways in which companies are using visual information to build a partnership for success. French management expert Michel Greif traveled throughout Europe and the United States studying how companies use visual communication and gathering materials for this book. Figure 1-4 presents a visual table of contents for the book, illustrating and summarizing the several major types of visual communication he has identified.

A visually identified team territory is the starting point. Work teams need to have a place they can identify as their own—a place to meet, to review indicators of the status of the work, to post information, to display personal touches and symbols of their team identity as well as examples of their product. Visual documentation encompasses ways of expressing the standard way to do the job so that new and experienced workers alike can produce even results. Although such documentation is often created by a technical department, it works best when its elements are first defined and refined by those who actually do the work.

Visual production control is already familiar to many readers in the form of kanban inventory systems. Greif's discussion brings in other types as well, including wall-size schedule charts and inventory control systems. Visual quality control includes alarm lamps for machine malfunctions, visual pass/fail templates for quick reading of gauges, charts generated by statistical process control methods, and records of every problem encountered.

Visual process indicators show the actual game score — the objectives and how the team is doing in meeting them. An important result of making this information visible and available to all is to objectify it. Rather than assigning blame, supervisors and workers together look at the situation and examine ways to improve it.

A visual factory also has visual mechanisms for tracking and celebrating progress and improvement. The author discusses CEDAC* as a key methodology for evaluating alternative solutions and reinforcing adherence to those that work. Other improvement-related topics discussed include an Idea Exchange for pooling and amplifying employees' ideas, and examples of companywide and departmental mission statements as continual reminders of the groups' ideals and progress.

Western companies must learn how to use visual information to align their employees' efforts with their overall goals and strategies. Our Japanese competitors are certainly doing it. The most remarkable plant I have ever visited was a Matsushita Washing Machine plant. The workers there knew the exact score, every moment of the day. Through visual systems, they knew exactly how much they needed to produce that day and where they were against the total. They knew how much cost saving any particular suggestion would produce. They knew the defect rate and how the quality of their work affected the quality of the final product. They recorded and posted every problem during the day, and they took pictures of each problem and the solution or improvement so that their ideas could stimulate other ideas. The result? The Matsushita Washing

---

* CEDAC is the registered service mark of Productivity, Inc.

Machine plant boasts a defect rate of *zero* — not one defect leaves the plant.

Is information powerful? You bet it is, and how much more powerful when shared with the people who can make the difference. I urge you to study this book carefully, discuss it in manager's groups, cross-functional team meetings, and work team gatherings. Find out what you can do to make sure all your teammates know the score.

I would like to thank Michel Greif for making his insightful book available to the English-reading audience and Productivity Press vice president Steven Ott for bringing the English edition into print. Bruce Hamilton, the vice president of manufacturing for United Electric Controls Company, winner of the 1990 Shingo Prize for manufacturing excellence, has prepared a fine foreword for the book. In addition to the companies mentioned in Dr. Greif's acknowledgments, a number of individuals deserve recognition for their contributions: Translator Larry Lockwood captured the warmth of the original. Gwendolyn Galsworth of Productivity, Inc., and Paul Everett of Simpson Timber offered valuable comments on the discussion of the CEDAC system. Karen Jones managed the editorial development of the project, and Marie Cantlon managed final manuscript preparation with the assistance of Mary Jane Curry (copyediting) and Aurelia Navarro and Jennifer Cross (proofreading). Joyce Ananian produced the index. David Lennon managed production of the book, which was designed and typeset by the staff of Rudra Press.

Norman Bodek
President
Productivity, Inc.

Preface

Beyond the bridge at Tancarville, the road bends to the right and continues beneath the chalk cliffs bordering the bed of the Seine. Driving next to the canal, one arrives at the Sandouville plant in a few minutes. There, inside large white buildings, is where the Renault group produces its top-of-the-line automobiles.

As a professor I often visit factories, either to accompany groups of students or business people or to pursue research. There is always something to see in exploring these contemporary monuments that manufacture the products that surround us — automobiles, clothing, frozen food, books, furniture, medications, and so on. There are presses for stamping, bending machines for twisting, machine tools for finishing, and tanks for mixing. Hundreds of small containers filled with colored parts travel between different assembly locations. Items travel overhead, hanging from conveyors as sinuous as rollercoasters. There is a pungent aroma of hot oil, an atmosphere electrified by sparks, and the powerful scent of plastics.

Yet I often found factory visits boring. It took me a while to grasp that I was bored because the inner meaning of the events occurring at different work areas eluded me — just as it probably eludes most of the people who work in factories.

Is production efficient or inefficient? Are steps being taken to improve quality or to reduce the level of malfunctions? Have inventory-reduction efforts been successful? Are production schedules and goals always met? Do workers participate in projects for improving production?

To answer these questions, we must enter the offices. There, one enters a dense forest of abstractions, as if abstractions were the only way of rendering the process of production meaningful. Most plants are tedious to visit because the reality of production is not visible at the point where production occurs. The work areas are like bodies without souls.

My visit to the plant at Sandouville lasted an entire day. Driving back toward Paris that night, I experienced an unusual feeling. Sandouville was different from most other factories. A sense prevails that its work areas are lived in. An inhabited area is more than an assortment of objects brought from other locations. A human presence is recognizable on initial contact. It is as if each personal touch, each color, each proportion speaks for the occupants.

Where does the sense of this human presence at the Sandouville plant originate? Is it the appearance of machines painted with different colors for each section? Or the routes marked on impeccably clean floors? Or the demonstration stands situated in the center of the work areas? Or instructional photographs placed near machines? Or large graphs showing performance data for the month? Or colored charts indicating the steps for solving technical problems? Or photographs explaining recent machinery improvements that various production teams have implemented?

An intimate relationship between my feeling of being in a lived-in factory and the composition of visual space within the factory was obvious, and my interest in visual organization therefore increased.

The theme of visual communication, however, has seldom been discussed in literature of industrial communication. The approach is dominated by an essentially technical outlook in which the medium for any given message is assumed to be socially and psychologically neutral. The essential objective is to communicate information bits in an economical and reliable way. That communication currents flow within factories like subterranean rivers is unimportant to traditional communication in the workplace.

Because I did not find a complete response to my questions in the literature, I pursued research related to visual communication in factories. I allocated a sabbatical year to develop documentation, visiting many plants and meeting people who could increase my knowledge.

In this year, I traveled throughout the world, visiting a large number of plants in France and other countries as I accumulated hundreds of examples directly from factory work areas.

I was struck by an initial observation: visual communication can also yield unsuccessful results. In some plants, I saw yellowed posters, bulletin boards covered with dust, graphs as motionless as antique clocks, and work areas left cluttered with empty boxes that were seldom repainted. Although management had sought to provide a new look in these plants, it had encountered unyielding obstacles.

One day a plant manager said, "Your idea is marvelous. Our steering committee had actually been looking for a way to motivate workers while informing them about their performance levels. We are going to put up graphs of productivity and quality levels in the work areas."

Because I was very familiar with this plant, I knew that communication was extremely underdeveloped there. From one day to the next, did this manager, with many good intentions, hope to convert a communications wasteland into a realm of signs? I expressed my skepticism. Not only were there few chances of succeeding with the project, but there was the risk that the employees would permanently reject any form of visual information. In this situation, the manager would forfeit the advantages that visual communication provides for firms whose projects are successful.

After my research visits, I established an initial conclusion derived from the repeated observation of a specific relationship: Every company that introduced visual communication was also pursuing significant changes in its modes of management and organization.

Thus, I came to recognize that visual communication is not merely a form of communication, comparable to other forms. Setting up a computer network, developing a system for routing interdepartmental memoranda, or creating an in-house newspaper is possible in any company. In an attempt to implant a visual communication system within a structure where certain principles are not upheld, however, the most probable outcome will be rejection.

The topic began to acquire another dimension. The initial questions that I had wanted to answer were technical in nature: How should one set up a bulletin board? What kind of information should be included? How should graphs be designed? Where should one put documents?

New questions were beginning to emerge: Why do certain types of organization facilitate the use of visual communication? What requirements need to be met for people to be interested in charts? What are the probable obstacles? How will an organization's chain of command be affected? Who should participate in defining visual space? Can visual communication work on a limited scale, or do rules of coherence require a company to rely on it to the fullest extent once it has been introduced? And what does "to the fullest extent" mean?

Thus I decided that instead of selecting visual communication in factories as a topic for my book, I should explore visual management of factories. This title reflects an important concept: The objective is not to introduce a system of visual communication, but *to create a visual mode of organization.*

THE VISUAL FACTORY

Building Participation
Through Shared Information

1

Visual Communication

In the era of the human conquest of space, the betrothal of computers and telecommunications has been celebrated with considerable fanfare. Futurologists have predicted that video-conferencing, long-distance computer networks, cable-communication systems, and telephones with video transmission will overcome distances almost miraculously.

But change sometimes emerges from unexpected sources. While we set our sights on creating more advanced communication technologies and installing powerful computers in our factories, an ancient mode of communication is being reborn—visual communication.

When did visual communication arise? Was it when armies began to be recognized by their banners? Or when hunters began carving notches in the butts of their muskets to indicate performance? Or when a community carved its creed on the walls of its temple? Or did visual communication emerge earlier, in an age when hunting methods were painted on the walls of caves?

Visual communication is not new. This ancient invention is spreading through the factories of the world like a trail of gunpowder. Visual communication is developing to the extent that within a few years people who visit factories that lack visual messages may feel that they are entering facilities darker than others.

Factories are truly in need of a revolution in communication. Traditional methods — departmental memoranda, reports, telephones, computer terminals — do not suffice. The channels are overloaded, information is garbled, the environment is saturated, and costs are out of control.

New communication needs are emerging. These needs originate with the desire to produce more efficiently and to deliver product to clients more quickly, with flawless quality, and at the most competitive price. These challenges are impossible to meet without developing ways of working more effectively.

While it is vital to meet these new communication needs, the solution will not come solely from technology, since the problem is not technological. Being able to send telecopier transmissions to Europe will not prevent the finishing division from being unfamiliar with the assembly division's activities. Nor will the presence of advanced computers in work areas prevent workers from throwing away accounting statements unanalyzed. In today's factories, the problem is how to communicate effectively at close range, not over long distances.

We have been looking in the wrong direction for answers. We were waiting for long-distance communication, but close-up communication is what we needed — ordinary communication, capable of facilitating daily work in familiar environments. Simple communication that is accessible to everyone promotes greater efficiency, which is what factories need today.

One usually thinks of visual communication as televised communication, audiovisual methods, or visual images. In ordinary speech, the word "visual" evokes a way of portraying concepts. The photographs and illustrations within this book are thought of as visual, but the text is not. Japanese writing with ideograms is visual; writing with an alphabet is not. This distinction between visual and written communication, however, does not encompass the range of visual communication in factories.

Assume that an illuminated panel with movable sections is to be installed in a work area. Although the message is transmitted in the form of a written text, this illuminated panel should be regarded as a component of our visual communication resources.

In an opposite example, the maintenance department is asked to furnish photographs of machines for the files. This use of a photograph does not engage us in visual communication, despite the visual nature of this way of portraying the machines.

The fact of exchanging information in factories by means of drawings and photographs is not the distinguishing mark of visual communication (although we will show that images are more effective than written messages). Rather, the way in which information is organized for accessibility is the distinguishing feature of visual communication in factories.

Visual communication is fundamentally an expression of visibility.

VISITS TO TWO WORKPLACES

To understand better the elements that characterize visual communication, consider two imaginary workplaces. These workplaces are similar in every respect, but one, the conventional workplace, employs traditional communication methods and the second, the visual workplace, uses visual communication. To endow this example with a certain degree of realism, assume that the two workplaces produce the same plastic components on the same type of injection-molding presses. After the components are molded, they are sent to another section of the plant to be assembled into finished products.

A Conventional Workplace

Let us enter the first workplace and approach one of the machines. The supervisor says to the operator, "We're behind schedule in producing the beige panels. We'll have to step up our work." How does the machine operator, who feels that he is working at a suitable pace, regard this message? The worker will likely think, "Of course. The supervisor had to invent some reason to make me speed up."

In the same workplace let us proceed to the supervisor's office. A note from the head of the inspection department is lying on the desk: "Many of the covers sent for assembly last month lacked the proper shape. Roger told me that twice as much time as usual was needed for attaching them." A skeptical response to a message about the unsuitable quality of something that one produces is a normal reaction — no one likes to be accused of creating problems. The supervisor will likely think, "That's impossible! We produced those parts just as we always do. Another excuse from the assembly department to explain one of its delays."

The telephone rings in the supervisor's office. The personnel office is replying to a machine operator's request to take a day off on May 14: "Impossible. Too much time off has been allowed already." The supervisor must convey this response to the worker, who will listen to the unpleasant news silently, while thinking, "The boss is holding a grudge because of my answer about speeding up those panels."

A Visual Workplace

Would the three messages be transmitted differently in a visual workplace? To find out, let us visit the other plant and approach the machines. The first object we notice is a board bearing two large messages written with a felt-tipped pen. (Figure 1-1) The first message is in red: "Friday, 12:00 p.m. 650 panels for the Vidal Co." The other message is in blue: "240 produced. Thursday, 6:00 p.m." It is obvious that there is a delay.

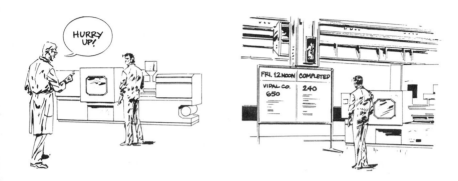

Figure 1-1. Two plants, two ways of communicating.

Anyone in this workplace can observe that achieving the goal will be difficult without remedial measures.

Let us continue our investigations and approach a panel near the rear of the work area, close to where the staff holds meetings. (Figure 1-2) A curve outlined with colored tape indicates trends for a particular quality indicator, namely, the percentage of parts accepted by the assembly department. Toward the middle of the month, this curve suddenly dipped, as indicated by the symbol of a small sun hidden by a cloud indicating "lousy weather."

When the assembly department encountered difficulties with parts made in the wrong shape, it immediately notified the production unit. The curve displayed provides a visible indication of the situation. Quality has declined undeniably.

On the basis of these signs, the machine operator visited his counterpart in the assembly department to learn about the difficulties. "There's no doubt. Roger can't get by with what's being delivered to him," he reported when he returned. Investigations began immediately to find the cause of the defect and to develop a solution.

Figure 1-2. Two plants, two ways of communicating.

Finally, in order to understand the way in which a visual workplace expresses the third message responding to the request for time away from work, we approach a board divided into two sections, with a "Work-Force Planning" heading. (Figure 1-3) The right side displays photographs of the entire group. On the left a curve records work attendance. To a certain extent, the board provides a schedule for the group for the next three months. Each member has indicated the days when he or she will be allowed to be absent. Thus, a glance at the curve is enough to tell the machine operator that if he is absent from work on May 14, the work force curve will drop below an acceptable level.

The machine operator will not be happy when he encounters this difficulty, but he will perceive the situation in a different manner. It is not that the supervisor refuses, but the situation creates a need. There are rules, which are the same for everyone. Moreover, the rules are posted. Everyone knows the normal work-force level and can see by consulting the performance curve that it becomes more difficult for the group to function below a certain level. "I know that if I let the group down, our performance levels for this month will go into the red," thinks the machine operator.

Two Perceptions of Reality

These three simple examples of everyday communication — a production delay, a problem with quality, and denial of a request for time away from work — have been contrasted to show specific features of visual communication. In each instance, the message is the same, but perceptions are different. If we were asked to define simply the nature of this difference, we might use words such as "objectivity," "reality," and "sharing."

Visual communication gives groups of people more accurate perceptions of reality.

COMMUNICATION WITH A SHARED PERSPECTIVE

The charts under discussion are large, with a reason: They must be visible at a distance.

Figure 1-3. Two plants, two ways of communicating.

Whereas in a conventional workplace, the operator of the 550-ton press may be the only person who is informed about a delay with the beige covers, in a visual workplace everyone is able to be aware of this problem by glancing at the production chart. Whereas in a conventional workplace, the supervisor is the only recipient of quality control reports, in a visual workplace everyone becomes aware of problems that the assembly department experiences. Whereas a request for time away from work constitutes personal information in a conventional workplace, the individual request becomes part of the information an entire group needs in a visual workplace.

The distinctive aspect of visual communication is that it is intended for a group, and not just for an individual. The consequences of this point are so important that it deserves to be emphasized.

The word "group" needs to be defined more precisely, because a group is one of the aspects that accounts for the originality of communication with a shared perspective. Sharing always involves an open group.

The concept of an open group of recipients is derived from the nature of the visual medium. A visual message is not restricted to a group of precisely identified individuals or specialists, or to a particular level of a hierarchy. A visual message is observed by everyone working in a given area, everyone who passes through the area, and, indeed, everyone who comes into the range of visibility.

To gain access to a message, however, observation is not enough. The meaning must also be understood. Nevertheless, comprehension is not limited by hierarchical positions or by specialized skills, but by membership in a specific cultural community. This is one of the fundamental differences of visual communication in relation to traditional communication. The goal in visual factories is to enlarge this community to extend the range of information to the largest number of people.

The advantages of this form of expansion are clear. Let's assume, for example, that a maintenance technician is responsible for preventive-maintenance procedures in a visual work area. She is there to render assistance. In a hierarchical sense, she is not under the authority of the area supervisor. There is nothing to prevent her from reading information included in the area's set of plans, however.

The maintenance technician can observe the schedule and the quantities that are being produced and cast a glance at the standard rates cited on the data sheet located near the machine. After quickly performing calculations, the technician tells her co-workers: "Don't push it too hard. You'll never meet your goals that way. Why don't you mount the die for covers on the 850-ton unit that operates twice as fast? Is that a problem? The attachments don't work? Don't worry about it. I'll set up a connecting piece right now, and the 650 covers will be ready for tomorrow."

Is the goal ambitious? Of course. Moreover, it is easy to anticipate that obstacles arise in plants where concealment of information prevails, or in organizations where some people are too proprietary about their knowledge.

If we try to establish visual communication in a firm with a rigid hierarchy and watertight structures, to communicate visually in the all-too-frequent context where a manager is someone who possesses knowledge that others lack, and to implement these recommendations where information continues to be a key to authority, we are bound to fail.

Visual communication is, above all, a matter of company culture, a culture where the essential principle is sharing. Hence, it is not coincidental that organizations that adhere to communication with a shared perspective also promote other forms of sharing: of space (teamwork, mobility), of tasks and responsibilities (job enrichment, participation in progress, decisions by consensus), and of values (acceptance of the firm's purposes and of its cultural identity).

SELF-SERVICE MESSAGES

During each visit to conventional workplaces, I receive a friendly greeting from the manager. I tell the manager about the visual plant. The manager sets up some visual devices — display boards, visual documentation, and the latest type of electronic boards. Technically, this plant now looks like a visual workplace.

To observe whether the new form of communication has yielded the anticipated improvements, let's approach the machines and listen to some candid comments. Let's talk with the operator of a 550-ton press. "650 panels for Friday at noon. The people in scheduling are still confusing dreams with reality! I do what I can. In fact, let me tell you something. Indicating the amounts we produce isn't such a bad idea. It's not foolish at all — from their standpoint. They can put on even more pressure, while we have all the headaches!"

Now let's look at the graph that presents the indicators for the work area. A machinist shares his views: "It's been just about two months since those boards were put up. What's new? OK, the managers visit our work areas more often. Look at that curve. That's how they can check our errors more easily. Those graphs let them see whether we're keeping up the pace. And the charts over there show whether we use too much oil and whether too many of us are absent."

Last, we approach the exit. There, we can see that the plant's managers have performed well. A colorful poster of the company charter is mounted in an elegant case. It begins: "As employees who are proud to work for the X Company, we affirm that our goal is customer satisfaction," and continues by citing the advantages of group efforts, mutual loyalty, and so on.

The proud employees of the X Company say: "Oh, yeah. They put up this poster one day when the chairman of the board visited the plant with some Japanese clients."

Indeterminate Recipients

Disheartened by the results? Analysis of this particular failure, however, yields an important observation: When a visual message is transmitted, one can never be certain that it will reach the intended recipient. An individual may not receive a message intended for an open group when the message, by definition, is not personally addressed.

Has anyone ever been able to force another to be interested in a display of graph curves? Has anyone ever been able to compel machine operators to glance quickly at the parts supply to determine whether the quantity is about to drop below the warning level? Has anyone ever been able to oblige machine operators to inform the maintenance department that a compressor is vibrating abnormally, if the operators believe that this device is not explicitly within the scope of their responsibilities?

The difficulty is readily recognizable. It is an integral component of the essence of visual communication, or the effort to promote systematic expansion of the group of recipients. When people are not personally involved, they can always believe that the information is intended for coworkers, supervisors, quality-control personnel, technicians, or management, and that there are no messages pertaining directly to them.

Messages in Search of Authors

The situation where the company displays its mission statement is instructive. By displaying this text — and using a plural "we" — the firm's management nurtured a vague hope that employees would feel that the document was intended for them. A shattered hope — the message was perceived as a speech for the world at large. Displaying it accomplished absolutely nothing. More effective — or at least less ambiguous — would have been to distribute an official memorandum.

Let us consider another example. The unit supervisor has written a number on the bulletin board: "650 panels for 12:00 p.m. Friday." To determine the effectiveness of this procedure we must ask: "Will the group be mobilized to achieve this goal?"

The reply rests on an essential condition: For the group to be mobilized, each member, seeing the quantity that has been indicated, must be convinced that he or she could have used the felt-tipped pen to write the goal on the boards. Everyone must be able to say, "That is our objective."

The supervisor is the author of the message when he or she records the objective. At the same moment, however, the supervisor must cease to be the author. If he or she had wished to write this production objective as a command — by personally appropriating visual space without respecting its laws — it would have been more effective to issue a directive.

In other words, if the quantity being indicated is not decided by prior consensus — a process examined in Chapter 4 — visual communication is not occurring. Rather conventional communication is occurring by means of posted announcements. The same phenomenon exists for technical data sheets placed near machines. They are only truly included within visual space — thereby ceasing to represent the supervisor's ideas — when anyone, upon reading a technical data sheet, is capable of imagining himself or herself its author.

The Self-service Principle

The problems of indeterminate recipients and messages in search of authors show clearly that visual communication is distinctive, since it is based on a fundamental change in the relationship between people and information, in fact, a reversal.

Visual communication is in conflict with traditional communication in this respect, too: It always depends on our intentions and wishes. We are never the *intended* recipients of visual messages; we *become* recipients of the messages that pertain to us. Likewise, we are never the authors of visual messages; we become authors of the messages that we accept.

Visual communication is based on intention. It works when one wants to become a recipient.

Recently, many plants have adopted a new form of production management. The Japanese call it self-service management. One process asks an earlier process for the parts it needs or sends a *kanban* ticket, which performs the same task. These visual production control techniques, including kanban tickets, are discussed in Chapter 4. A machine operator selects the needed components from the storage area for the workplace.

Visual communication embodies the same principle: self-service communication. For example, machines with flashing warning lights, photographs offering recommendations for avoiding errors, a proposed improvement indicated in a neighboring group's progress chart — these items are available to meet each worker's needs. Messages are received according to whether or not readers regard themselves as clients for information. If no one pays attention to a message, it should be removed from circulation after a time.

Defining recipients of visual messages as clients — persons who are free to receive information or not — may appear slightly exaggerated. In some instances, such as safety instructions, there is limited room for discussion, but the concept is the same. Visual information must meet needs. The information client, not the supplier, is the one who controls visual communication.

Thus it is no coincidence that development of a new visual medium closely resembles a marketing campaign. In some plants, project managers working on visual display systems talk about research on needs, testing, an introductory campaign, and promotional efforts. The use of this type of language is extremely revealing.

An Environment Organized Like Public Property

The self-service image provides the correct orientation. The next phase provides confirmation: Visual communication is the predominant mode of communication within organizations that seek to reinforce employee autonomy.

For some people, the word "autonomy" evokes an image of withdrawal and isolation from the rest of the organization. When the concept of autonomy is examined within this book, however, isolation and withdrawal do not come into play. Instead, the emphasis is on openness, expansion of contacts, and greater cohesion.

Moreover, it is not accidental that the self-management groups that emerged in some companies during the sixties did not use visual communication. The autonomy of these closed and self-sufficient groups was distinguished by a low level of interaction and integration with the rest of the plant. Communication with others was not an urgent need for them.

The autonomy associated with visual communication is oriented toward enriching relationships, not weakening them. This autonomy is analogous to the autonomy of travelers, who are able to move, to interpret particularly expressive environments, and to maintain relations with the inhabitants according to their respective roles and the immediate situation. Augustin Berque[1], in evoking an individual's ability to interact with his or her milieu, uses the term "allonomy," and has shown that this form of autonomy is widespread in Japan.

The traveler analogy explains why the visual factory so closely resembles an urban landscape. As we pass through the work areas, we sometimes have an impression of walking in a city, or driving along a public thoroughfare. Respecting the rules of the road, checking the time by a public clock, catching a train

---

[1] Augustin Berque, *Vivre l'espace au Japon*, (Paris: Presses Universitaires de France, 1982).

in a railway station, strolling through the open areas of an exhibition, driving a leased vehicle, making one's way through a self-service store, or consulting a catalog at home: All of these actions resemble activities performed today in visual factories.

An era has ended. Feudal factories are behind us. In the plants of tomorrow, space will be organized like public property.[2]

COMMUNICATION WITH TOTAL VISIBILITY

Compared with a conventional workplace, messages become more convincing, more objective, and more faithful to reality in a visual workplace. What mechanism accounts for this quality? Is it merely the presence of physical objects?

In ordinary speech, we often say "You have to see it to believe it." When a person says, "It's clear to see," he or she is expressing the idea that reality is involved. Apart from the physical objects — machinery or parts — that can be observed in a work area, certain abstract messages are also regarded as being more real when they are expressed visually. Why does a curve that is displayed on a chart seem more real than a departmental memorandum?

---

[2] The expressions "feudal factory" and "public property" are not used without justification. The rise of visual factories marks the abandonment of a system where authority is based on the hoarding of information and on the absolute right of the hierarchy to establish laws (in the form of methods, rules, and objectives). It is a mode of organization where information is shared and where methods, rules, and objectives are developed through a consensus-based process. This transformation is similar to the process which historically contributed to the rise of the modern state. More specifically, in the situation under examination, the latter process led to the appearance of a public domain defined as locations where, as Kant expressed it, "the public consensus of reasoning people" can exist. Consult Jürgen Habermas, *L'Espace public* (Paris: Editions Payot, 1978), as well as Louis Quéré, *Des miroirs equivoques* (Paris: Editions Aubier, 1982).

To answer this question, we must return to the conventional workplace. Since our last visit, management has tried to make communication more objective and not another form of control. Now messages transmit nothing but facts.

The following information appears on a large illuminated board: "The 550-ton press is behind schedule with the beige panels." "Last month's Quality Control Department report: The assembly unit received 60 unsuitable covers." "Request for time off on May 14 not approved: personnel shortage."

Progress has occurred, although the factory is still different from a visual workplace. Messages are treated in an isolated manner in a conventional workplace; they are disseminated in a miserly way, as if they were expected to be sufficient in and of themselves. In a visual workplace, on the other hand, messages are systematically placed within a larger and more tangible context.

To say "The 550-ton press is behind schedule" is one thing; to provide a continuous visual indication of the status of quantities being produced in relation to a commitment is another. To say "The assembly unit received 60 misshapen covers" is one thing; to gain day-to-day familiarity with the client's problems — by visiting the client when necessary — is something else. To say "Request for time off denied: personnel shortage" is one thing; to display a schedule for absences next to the work-force-planning principles approved by the group is something else.

Although it is tempting to believe that a visual workplace disseminates more messages than a conventional workplace, the concept of a quantitative increase itself is misleading. The difference does not come from quantity (ten illuminated boards that disseminate only certain kinds of messages cannot change anything). A complete change of approach separates the two modes of communication. In conventional communication, information is transmitted. In visual communication, nothing is transmitted: One creates an information field and organizes the employees' access to this field.

In other words, a conventional workshop endowed with an electronic board may issue a few messages, but a visual workplace *enables people to see*. Whereas a conventional workplace retains the concept of hierarchical channels through which messages that are defined as "relevant" travel, a visual workplace is endowed with a communication structure whose nature is to allow everything that is meaningful to be seen and to provide meaning for everything that can be seen.

For this reason, the idea of "ascending," "descending," or "lateral" communication becomes meaningless in a visual workplace. Messages cease to travel. They are recorded in specific spaces. Information channels are replaced by information fields. The point where communication is totally visible and transmits neutral messages is where visual communication becomes capable of converting the visual landscape into a representative image of reality. There is no room for doubt. In a visual factory, the space actually speaks.

Returning to Earth

There are two consequences of a commitment to total visibility. First, visual communication allows everything that lends meaning to a given activity to become directly observable in a given area. Hence, the abundance of information that characterizes visual workplaces.

Has the group defined a productivity objective? Then the objective must be visible. Are operating personnel responsible for quality? Then quality must be visible. Must precise work instructions be followed? Then the instructions must be visible. Has a quality circle developed ideas? Then the ideas must be visible. Is the client satisfied? Then this satisfaction must be visible, too. If visual communication is a self-service situation, then it is necessary for the channels to be properly supplied. Hence the exceptional diversity of themes and visual messages that are at work in a visual setting.

The second consequence is derived from an opposite concept. If everything that can be seen within an area is by its very nature endowed with a specific meaning from the observer's viewpoint, it is difficult to deny visible evidence. Dust gathering on pallets is as valid an indicator for evaluating inventory levels as an inventory turnover coefficient. Observation of recurrent breakdowns on certain machines becomes as pertinent for determining financial profitability as the fixed-assets ratio on a balance sheet. The defective items ignored in the rear portion of a building offer a convincing refutation of the lyrical outpourings included in a recent treatise on total quality by the firm's management.

It is important to know. For management that has traditionally dealt solely in abstractions, to begin to pursue the path of visibility is to accept the principle of returning to reality.

A NEW ROLE FOR THE HIERARCHY

Institutional communication in conventional factories has developed according to the principle of congruency between the communication system and the organizational chart. Visual communication proposes another pattern — a visual field where the network for exchanging information is detached from the network for issuing orders.

This difference does not mean no more orders are to be executed, nor that certain information should not continue to flow through hierarchical channels, but only when circumstances justify these modes of communication. For every other situation, the hierarchical structure should forfeit its role as sole medium to a special medium that belongs to the entire group of employees, so that the communicative environment is similar to a public area intended for all citizens.

Naturally, many executives dread the notion of losing control of information. Why should they worry? If the owner of a small grocery store decides to mark aisles on the floor and provide signs to orient his customers, or installs display cases and labels the products, or installs a scale that automatically issues a price sticker for fruits and vegetables so that the store can become self-service, is the grocer thereby abandoning authority? Does the grocer cease to own the store because customers gain greater autonomy in relation to their environment?

Visual communication challenges the *mode* of expression adopted by hierarchical authority rather than the *form* of authority itself.

In traditional communication systems, the role of executives is to know everything, to centralize everything, and to control everything. Henceforth to ensure effective communication it will be necessary for them to proceed differently. They must encourage contact among members of different teams, create a need for information, develop means of adapting visible signs within a given area, and adopt measures to ensure that visual space will be properly sustained and accessible to employees. Management's responsibilities have expanded. Now it is necessary to create communication areas and to sustain them.

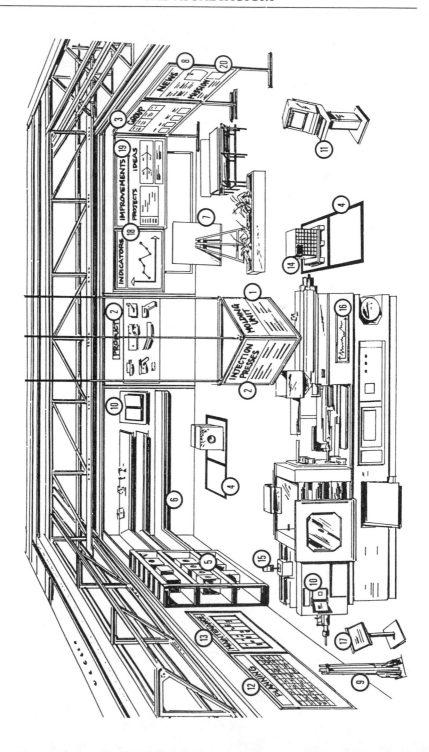

It would be somewhat paradoxical to speak of visual comunication without relying on an image. This is the reason for presenting a visual workplace in Figure 1-4.

The workplace depicted is not an archetype for visual work areas, nor a practical example to be followed literally. Each firm has its own constraints and operating structures. There is no reason automatically to include everything appearing in this sketch within the visual landscape of a plant. Conversely, other elements -- or other forms of presentation -- may be more suitable for certain situations. In this portrayal, the intent is to present significant visual communication themes that the book analyzes in detail.

The Team's Territory

1. Identification of territory
2. Identification of activities, resources, and products
3. Identification of the team
4. Markings on the floor
5. Marking of tools and racks
6. Technical area
7. Communication area and rest area
8. Information and instructions
9. Neatness (broom)

Visual Documentation

10. Manufacturing instructions and technical procedures

Visual Production Control

11. Computer terminal
12. Production schedule
13. Maintenance schedule
14. Identification of inventories and work-in-process

Visual Quality Control

15. Monitoring signals for machines
16. Statistical process control (SPC)
17. Record of problems

Displaying Indicators

18. Objectives, results, and differences

Rendering Progress Visible

19. Improvement activities
20. Company project and mission statement

Figure 1-4. A visual workplace.

2

A Team's Territory

The Fichet Bauche plant in Oustmarest, France, manufactures locks and other security products such as armored doors. Mr. Dumollard, who is responsible for operations, served as my guide on a visit.

"The flowers were the thing that surprised me the most," he confided when we entered the lock-assembly area. He continued:

> Our specialty is metalworking and assembly, not a very clean activity. When I arrived here on a Monday morning, I sensed something odd as soon as I entered the work area — a change in the atmosphere.
>
> Then I looked at the shelves, and I was astonished to see that the employees had put flowers beside the unassembled parts, which were perfectly arranged. Just some pots with red geraniums, which made me think of the houses in our area. You know, these little white houses with slate roofs and with flowers of various kinds on the balconies. The atmosphere was like a festival.

Why this change? Why, on a given morning, did the employees decide to decorate their work area without having been asked to? What was the unspoken message expressed in the language of flowers?

Two weeks earlier, the plant had changed its scheduling method to achieve better organization. Before that, parts had been delivered to the assembly line according to the pace of the finishing units. The containers arrived haphazardly, creating nearly uncontrollable disorder in the assembly area. Now the workers were using kanban tickets to indicate their actual needs.[1]

The way the plant had functioned previously — with flows being pushed forward without any concern for the assembly unit's actual needs — had understandably kept the employees from feeling at home in the plant. What would you say if a store delivered your purchases ahead of schedule, claiming that its delivery trucks were free that day?

The example of Fichet Bauche shows that when employees gain some control over their surroundings, or when they begin to feel that they are in a "home away from home," as I heard people say in an American plant, they begin to organize their visual environment. Flowers today, then some boards with work instructions and explanatory photographs, perhaps, and later, performance graphs.

A HABITABLE SPACE

A visual mode of organization cannot develop if employees are not free to adapt their surrounding space. Maintaining the commitments and results that are displayed in work areas (quality objectives, production schedules, inspection instructions, performance indicators) requires a close, familiar relationship with

---

[1] The Fichet Bauche plant's previous method was a "push-flow" method, which aims to maximize instantaneous activity at each work location. The new method is a "pull-flow" method, which allows improvement of general conditions (flexibility, reliability of deliveries, overall productivity). Under the influence of Japanese industry, many plants in Western nations are adopting this mode of operation. The transformation requires extensive changes, both technical and cultural.

the setting where these messages will appear. To want to express themselves in an environment, people must feel at home.

My observations in factories confirm this point. Visual communication cannot develop in the absence of a mode of organization that offers employees a space they can treat as theirs. This space is a "territory."

Territory is an identified milieu intended for a production process, where one or more production teams pursue their activities.[2] The conditions that render a given setting a habitable territory are described throughout the remainder of the book. One condition that deserves emphasis is that the production team be systematically involved in decisions concerning organization of its space.

Whether it is a matter of placing a chart on a board, creating a new storage area, controlling production flows (as in the case of Fichet Bauche), or changing the positions of machines, the golden rule of visual organization is to ensure participation by the people who use a given location.

TEAM TERRITORY

Figure 1-4 shows only one machine and no one working. Let us add a few people and have the machine represent several machines. But how many people and how many machines? Does the figure depict an extremely large work area for three

---

[2] When work is done by assigned teams (morning and afternoon shifts, for example), several groups must share the same territory. The same board may contain information intended for various teams. Distinctions among teams are shown with different colors. According to the production manager at the Valeo plant near Le Mans, France, this situation does not entail any specific problems: "Each team shares resources just as partners owning a sailing vessel would. The important goal is for maintenance of the ship to be performed according to the rules."

hundred people, or a work area for two or three employees, or a small unit with twelve members?

The answers to these questions are important, for responsiveness to information depends on an individual's identification with the particular level of the organization. One does not react in the same way to individual results as to boards placed at the main entrance of a plant to indicate companywide performance.

Visual communication organizes information according to several levels, from individual work stations to the entire factory or firm, while including sections, shops, or departments. Nevertheless, the central level for organizing information is the basic work unit or "production team." The size varies according to the specific technology, but usually includes six to twenty members.

The highest density of visual messages is always observed on the production-team level. Communication with a shared perspective appears to be the preferred mode of expression within the team, and also between teams and the rest of the organization.

Visual communication depends on a sharing process; a team is the first level of the organization where sharing occurs. The precise function of a team is to operate certain machines, to achieve collective goals, and to be involved in the outcome. A team's territory is the fundamental location for the collective sharing of visual information. The team's territory occupies the role of a basic channel in a conventional communication network; it is a unit connected to every other unit, an essential link in the system of information exchange.

Is it impossible, then, for a company that has not adopted a teamwork structure to use visual communication effectively? The answer is conditional. Indeed, the concept of teamwork allows multiple interpretations. In some instances, the term pertains to groups whose daily activities are extremely autonomous. In other instances, teamwork suggests weekly meetings to stay abreast of current problems; elsewhere it refers to quality circles or multidisciplinary planning groups.

This variety of situations prevents me from giving a categorical answer. The intensity of the exchanges of communication is more decisive than the mode of organization. In a traditional structure, where each operator is isolated without direct contact with other members of the group, it is difficult for a visual mode of communication to be effective. For visual communication to thrive, the team's territory must become an area for intensive interaction.

A MEETING PLACE

The term "territory" usually evokes the idea of a protected area, where one retreats from an attack, and where access is difficult for anyone who does not belong. Nothing could be farther from the essence of totally visible communication than being enclosed in one's territory. Visual messages are always simultaneously intended for both internally and externally directed communication. This dual function — which may involve intricate problems of spatial arrangement at the point when charts containing indicators must be displayed — is one of the requirements for success with visual organization.

When messages are excessively directed toward a group's internal needs rather than toward external communication, the group soon regards "official visualization" as unnecessary. In this case, informal interpretation of indicators or verbal communication based on the group's internal codes appears to be more effective.

Conversely, if the messages are most useful for people outside the group, the team will steadily lose interest and cease to regard boards or charts as among its working tools.

The visual territory is characterized by a certain dualism, existing simultaneously as a basis for the group's cohesion and as a unifying nexus within the organization. In the final analysis, the visual territory is a house, but a house that is oriented toward a town. The Fichet Bauche employees arranged flowers in their workplace, like people decorating the porches of their homes.

A mode of organization that facilitates visual communication is comparable to such mixed public/private territories as porches.[3]

The fact that a team's territory may be an area that is both open and closed has practical implications for selecting locations for visual resources. The placement of visual aids always expresses a symbolic message at a secondary level. We will examine this concept in relation to two examples from plants of the Télémécanique and Valeo companies.

A Public Commitment

The Télémécanique plant in Carros, France, employs 200 people. The plant produces programmable robots as well as electronic devices for industry. Employee participation is a long-established tradition here, as it is throughout the Télémécanique group of companies. The mode of organization here is based on work in small groups that are responsible for their results and their progress.

As one enters the plant, it is clear that visual communication is highly developed. Instructions, schedules, results, and photographs of the group's accomplishments and progress can be seen at various work areas.

A maintenance schedule posted on a machine (Figure 2-1) is presented as a calendar showing the dates for scheduled maintenance. The operators perform certain routine maintenance

---

[3] In his book about space in Japan (*Vivre l'espace au Japon*, op. cit.), Augustin Berque emphasizes the role of borders in company organization, whereby "areas, boundaries, and contextual affinities are emphasized, in contrast to our approach, which emphasizes points, lines, and subsequent continuations." From Berque's book one concludes that — in conjunction with other factors — the Japanese predilection for communicating with posters can be explained by the existence of space organized by a logic based on surfaces.

procedures, but most of the work indicated on the calendar is not part of their responsibilities. This work is performed by the maintenance department.

The maintenance schedule was posted in this location for two reasons. The first is a practical measure: Everyone can be readily aware of the scheduled dates for shutting down the equipment for maintenance.

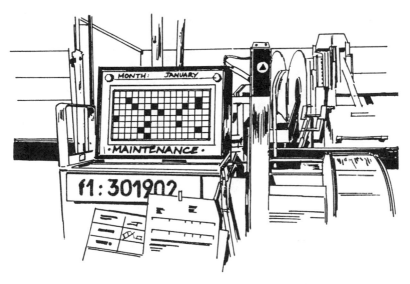

Figure 2-1. The Télémécanique plant at Carros, France. Maintenance schedule posted on a machine.

The second reason is symbolic. By placing the schedule near the machine, the company is issuing a public announcement: "The production team uses this machine every day, and maintenance is performed by a specialized department that is not based in this work area. Both departments are responsible for proper operation of this machine. The only thing that counts is that the machine should not be idle." To reinforce this unspoken message, the schedule that was formerly kept in a technical area was placed on the machines in a spot where everyone can see it.

To understand the symbolism, I asked a team leader how production personnel perceive the presence of a document "belonging" to another department within their territory: "The operators meet with the technicians in front of that board on a regular basis," the team leader said. "If the scheduled maintenance may not take place during the specified week, the operators become concerned about the delay. It's like drivers concerned about their cars trying to extract promises from mechanics to do the right things at the right time."

The symbolic meaning appears frequently. It is encountered again with the production schedule and improvement projects organized by multidisciplinary groups. In a suitably designed visual structure, immediate visibility — or advertising — of objectives gives official endorsement to the commitments of both parties.

Depicting the Facts

The Valeo plant near Le Mans employs 900 people and produces temperature-control systems for automobiles (heating and air conditioning). During recent years, the plant has implemented a coherent plan to involve the entire work force in the functioning of the work areas. The plant is divided into territories known as "Autonomous Production Areas." The employees are organized according to "Autonomous Production Groups," one or more of which pursue their activities within each autonomous production area. The result of these reorganization measures has been an astounding increase in efficiency.

The line on the graph in Figure 2-2 indicates changes in a quality indicator for the unit where radiators are produced. The

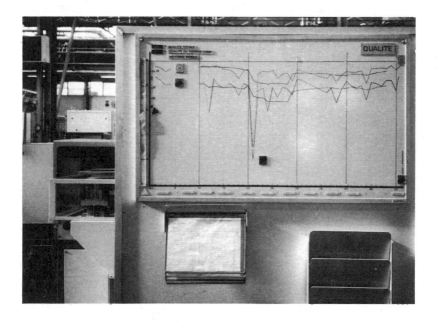

Figure 2-2. The Valeo plant at La Suze-sur-Sarthe, France. Performance indicators.

graph faces the main passageway, rather than the interior of the unit's territory.

Observing the shape of the line, we see a sharp decline at the beginning of the second quarter. This decline represents a decrease in quality. What is the team's attitude toward this less than impressive performance that is openly displayed?

If such a chart is displayed in a plant where in the event of poor performance the first reflex is to hunt for a someone to blame, the group will feel that it is being trapped. On the one hand, displaying the indicator chart emphasizes the group's acceptance of responsibility for its results. On the other hand, the group is aware — as is everyone — that in any factory very few results depend solely on an individual or a small group.

If quality has declined, it is possible that the material was too damp, or that a machine was improperly adjusted by a technician, or that the quality-control department had not properly calibrated its instruments. Whenever someone feels under attack, excuses are easy to find.

Why, therefore, would a team allow the public display of unfavorable results? Why would it agree to turn its face outward and perhaps to lose face as a result?

There is only one answer. The displaying of results at the scene of activities plays an extremely precise role — the expression of facts, without pointing a finger. This neutrality gives visual communication its power. Displaying the information allows departments an opportunity to meet in response to objective reality.

This point offers an insight into the relationship between a team in a given territory and the charts placed there. The performance criteria expressed by the indicators do not pertain to performance by the team. They relate to performance by a production unit controlled by the team. This distinction of only a few words is enormously important. Regardless of levels of responsibility, everyone who has accepted a commitment (as with Télémécanique's maintenance schedule) or is responsible for a set of results (Valeo's performance indicators) must feel that the boards displayed in a territory are their concern.

A purchasing manager passing by a kanban board should be able to say, "Conditions have improved since we entered into a partnership with Company D." A technician from the research department passing by a curve indicating shortages, displayed in the storage area for parts, should be able to say, "Conditions have improved since we updated our classification system." A personnel manager passing by a maintenance schedule that has been perfectly upheld should be able to say, "Conditions have improved since we began to provide training."

As in a Formula One race, the mechanics do not actually sit behind the steering wheel. Nevertheless, throughout the race, they nervously pace back and forth, hoping for a win. When the cars pass the pit, it is as if the technicians, in their minds, were the drivers. Seeing together is being together.

An Area for Shared Responsibility

For a long time, companies were organized with a rigid separation of responsibilities. Staff departments found it difficult to allow production units to interfere with their functions, and, conversely, they were unwilling to become involved in the production units' functions.

This situation is changing. In many factories, production units are performing maintenance activities, and maintenance departments are becoming involved in production, often entrusting a portion of their duties to production units. On the other hand, staff departments are also assuming considerably greater responsibility for the smooth functioning of production units. As a result of these overlaps, a far cry from the "tend-your-own-garden" mode of organization, people are ceasing to worry about how much less they do and beginning to ask how much more they can do.

The physical presence of information is irreplaceable to the process of covering responsibilities in the work area. Whereas people in their own offices are normally concerned only with responsibilities derived from their own positions, a shared responsibility for information that is observed emerges when several members of an organization meet in front of the board.

Visual territory is a meeting place. Within the theater of operations and in full view of concrete realities, attitudes change. Everyone assumes the role appropriate to the situation. Doers (producers) distance themselves slightly and become observers. Observers (specialists) engage themselves and to a certain extent become doers. Attempts at blaming and defending cease. Instead, there are joint efforts to find solutions, replacing rain clouds with sunshine.

Summary

1. Development of a visual mode of organization depends on the existence of a territory in which the employees feel a sense of ownership. This location is not exclusively held property, but rather displays the features of public property. This mixture of personal involvement and public access is key.
2. Visual communication develops in response to the frequency of two types of contact: within a small group (in the team's territory) and contact between the group and the rest of the organization (this is why a team's territory must be open space). Visual organization promotes team cohesion and incorporation of the team into the organization.
3. The position for visual messages expresses a twofold symbolic message:
   • Visibility of a message within an area of activity implies public sharing of responsibility by everyone who is at all involved in the activity.
   • The display of messages within a given territory embodies the presumption that those who perform actions are capable of distancing themselves from the visually portrayed information. Participants and observers must be able to approach one another on an equal plane, confronting objective realities that do not convey blame.

The second portion of this chapter explains some of the practical aspects of defining a territory — how to identify a territory and how to describe a team's activities and responsibilities — as well as discussing the importance of preparing a communication area and keeping the territory neat and well organized. The last portion of this chapter looks at the advantages offered by visitors to a visual factory.

IDENTIFYING A TERRITORY

To initiate a visual organization project, the first step is to identify a territory. By symbolically attributing individuality to a territory, the company provides the conditions necessary for using all of the communication resources that will be described later.

To make sure identification of a territory does not become isolated from the larger organization, avoid physically enclosing the area (unless technical conditions require it). An assembly line at the Renault plant in Sandouville, France, demonstrates that it is possible to create visual territory without extremely favorable conditions. (Figure 2-3)

Figure 2-3. The Renault plant at Sandouville, France

Symbolic boundaries are always preferable to actual enclosures: A simple panel hung from the ceiling to name the section and give a brief description of its activities is sufficient to create a territory. (Figure 2-4) Painted floors and shelves, distinctive wall decorations, the positioning of charts, and the identification of meeting and communication areas are also appropriate means of demarcating territory.

The objective is not to create a work of art, but to enable the team to feel that it is in a homelike environment. Thus, the members of the group must be responsible for selecting the decor, although appropriate departments can help and coordinate.

Figure 2-4. Identification of an assembly line unit at the Renault Sandouville plant. The board contains the names of unit supervisors, as well as brief descriptions of activities (mounting pipes beneath the chassis, gas tanks, and so on).

In some companies, a working group representing multiple teams is responsible for investigating various possibilities, to provide the initial stimulus and to maintain a certain harmony of colors from group to group. Since each team may be have its own style, the company's identity could be highlighted by use of a particular color or a shared logo.

An Example

The way in which territories were created along the assembly line at the Renault plant in Sandouville is instructive. An automobile assembly line is one form of organization truly ill suited — even resistant — to division into subgroups. Imagine an uninterrupted succession of stations assembling a vehicle along a five-hundred meter path. Physical division of the line is unimaginable.

Nevertheless, the line in the Renault factory was symbolically divided into territories. Each territory is allocated to a group of approximately 20 assembly workers, coordinated by a supervisor. At Sandouville, these groups are called "units." Specific responsibilities for quality, costs, personnel training, organizing of work stations, and participation in improvements are allocated to these units.

The identity of a territory is easily recognizable. Each area is painted with a specific color (floor, furnishings, items of equipment) that sets it apart from other units.

After this new organization was introduced at Sandouville, contact within the group was significantly reinforced, and visual communication appeared. (Figure 2-3) Apart from the information panel, the communication space contains a rest area and a meeting area as well as various resources that reflect the activities of the group. We will discuss these resources (a board for recording and analyzing problems, a suggestion box, and the like) later.

IDENTIFYING LOCATIONS

In certain plants, no indicators, reference points, or maps help people find their way. The initial impression is of an old plant where everyone knows the layout by heart. Everyone is aware that cutting is performed at the old forge, that accessories are kept in the upper storage area, and that sheet metal is stored behind the large aisle.

Experience teaches that knowledge is never shared so effectively. Many workers never set foot outside their own section; they are ignorant of the names or the functions of other work areas.

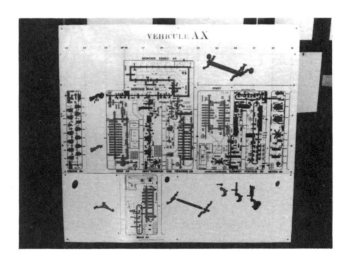

Figure 2-5. Map at Citroën plant, Caen, France. Technical floorplans are usually unsuitable as maps intended for public communication. The maps should be clear and attractive. This plant, which manufactures mechanical connecting components, adopted a map in which production units are represented by colors and the processing areas are represented by drawings of the principal products manufactured in those areas. Other plants likewise include physical flow patterns in their maps, using lines of different colors and photographs of the products.

When locations are changed infrequently and the layout is stable, public identification of various areas is unnecessary. On the other hand, when a plant must welcome new workers, or when the layout and personnel assignments change frequently, everyone should be able to identify locations easily.

Ignorance of the layout of a plant becomes a significant handicap when an employee needs to transport parts or documents in person, to meet with a client, or to attend a meeting. Some decentralized methods of production control also cannot be applied in the absence of perfectly clear sets of signals.

Implementing a signage project following the example of our cities is easy. Techniques such as street markings, maps, identification of monuments, and use of colors to differentiate locations according to their nature can be transposed unadapted to a factory milieu to identify inventories, tool storage areas, passageways, and so on. Many techniques can help everyone interpret and understand the environment and increase employees' mobility.[4]

DESCRIBING ACTIVITIES, RESOURCES, AND RESPONSIBILITIES

In certain factories, the number and variety of descriptive panels sometimes convey the impression of a public exhibition hall. Who are these explanations concerning machines, products, and technologies for? Are they intended solely for visitors?

---

[4] Production managers often complain that employees do not like to change work locations. Among the many factors that hinder mobility (classifications, salary levels, and so on), are those that stem from the difficulty in orienting oneself in an unfamiliar environment. Every frequent traveler who stays in international hotel chains is aware of this issue. Being in a familiar context, or at least in a context that is easy to interpret, greatly facilitates changing locations. The relationship between mobility and communication will be discussed in Chapter 3.

At the Hewlett-Packard computer plant in Cupertino, California, a manager provided an interesting answer:

> Our descriptive panels offer three advantages:
>
> - First we consider it indispensable for new members of our work force — whether recently hired or transferred from another team — to understand what they are producing. Not just the procedure, but the entire process, as well as the technology and the product. They should be capable of situating what they are doing in relation to the other teams upstream and downstream in their sections. Because of the panels, any member of a team can assume responsibility for informing a new person very quickly. In addition, seeing the names of machines and procedures in writing helps the newcomer learn the group's terminology.
> - Second, the panels facilitate visiting. By relying on visual explanations, anyone can act as a guide. This is convenient and time-saving.
> - Third, displaying information about someone's activities is a way of providing recognition. When other people understand what work you do, you feel much more important.

Like an emblem, the description of the activities, resources, and responsibilities affirms the identity and skills of those in a given territory. For instance, if there is an ℞ at the entrance to a store, everyone knows that a licensed pharmacist is available inside.

Practical Implications

What kind of information should be presented? What kind of media should be used and in how much detail? The answers depend on the individual company. Each company possesses its own management style, unique projects, and distinctive approaches as well as space limitations.

A coherent presentation usually includes:

- a succinct description of activities (Figure 2-6)
- an identification of the team (Figure 2-13)
- a description of technical and economic features of the resources and processes (Figures 2-8, 2-9, and 2-10)

Some companies go even further. They prepare panels of diagrams and photos that depict the appropriate technology and manufacturing methods. Others provide descriptions of the business environment: the nature of the market, the firm's principal clients, and the nations to which it exports. In plants that have a total quality management approach, teams are often asked to define the relationships and service obligations that link them to internal or external clients and suppliers. (Figure 2-7)

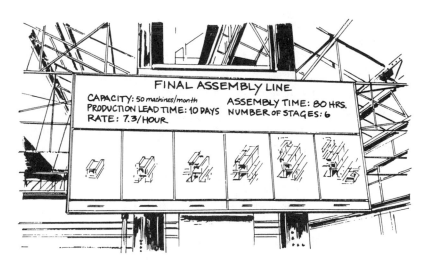

Figure 2-6. Explanation of the manufacturing process for a machine tool (over 12 feet long). (For legibility, only some of the eighteen steps described were reproduced in this sketch.)

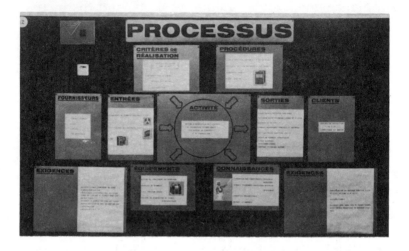

Figure 2-7. Display at the Bull plant, Angers, France. This team-created board shows information about the customers, suppliers, process, and improvements.

Seizing an Opportunity

Some companies take advantage of special events to launch campaigns to use signs and explanatory displays. Such events can include open-house days, the launch of new programs, zero defects days, anniversaries of plant openings, or repainting of buildings. There are multiple opportunities for enhancing the impact of a project.

A final suggestion: Take before-and-after photographs and mount them on a panel. If the plant's actual appearance has changed, the results can create a strong impression.

EXHIBITING PRODUCTS

Every organization possesses its own symbols. In factories, in most instances one sees only the machines. They seem to be proclaiming: "Admire us! We are the world's most powerful presses! We are the most advanced robots!" Why not exhibit

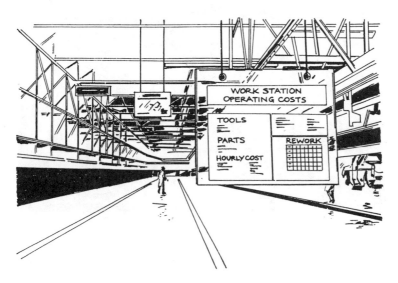

Figure 2-8. Operating cost chart at Renault plant, Sandouville.
Team members asked a supervisor for their assembly units to display the characteristics of the resources entrusted to them, at each position. ("We want to know the price of the equipment that we will be handling.") Small panels (approximately 40 cm. wide) have been put up along the assembly line. Various information appears on the panel for the operator of the screw-inserting machine: the designation of the equipment, technical characteristics of the machine, its purchasing price, and yearly upkeep. Other figures have been added: the cost of protective items used by the operator, the cost of one hour of rework, and the cost of a day when a workplace accident occurs.

products in work areas, too? Better than machines, products represent the purpose that unifies the various components of the company. Products symbolize everyone's efforts. (Figure 2-11)

If a plant manufactures intermediate products, link these components with the products that customers make with them. The J. Reydel company at its Gondecourt, France, plant has adopted this approach. (Figure 2-12) The firm considered it important to display its instrument products in the form in which the customers install them. Several boards have been mounted in the work area: People can view instrument panels

Figure 2-9. Citroën plant, Caen. A rack installed in a work area displays various phases of the stamping process on a transfer press line.

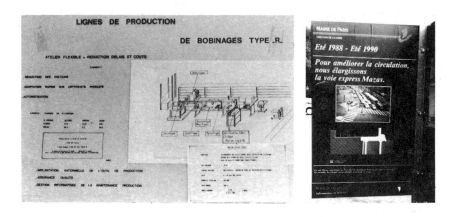

Figure 2-10. Explanatory panels at the Société Anonyme de Télécommunications plant in Lannion, France, (printed circuit and electronics manufacturers). When a machine-installation project is approved, an explanatory panel is placed at the location where the machine will be, in advance of the installation date.

This idea is similar to the signs a city posts to announce the nature and duration of a construction project, to identify construction that may inconvenience the public and will change the nature of community property. (The sign on the right reads, "Office of the Mayor of Paris — Summer, 1988 to Summer, 1990. To improve traffic flow we are widening the Mazas expressway.")

Figure 2-11. The Renault plant at Sandouville. Semi-finished vehicles on display in the body section.

as well as photographs and articles from publications about the vehicles for which these instruments are made. In this way, the customer is symbolically present at the workplace.

IDENTIFY THE TEAM

On a visit to the Hewlett-Packard plant in Greeley, Colorado, I entered the work area of a group now known as "Pomponeety" (a combination of the nicknames of the mixed-model line's three products — "Pompeii," "le moineau," and "tweety"). First-level manager Dawn Parker proudly showed me the team's communication board. Each member's name and photograph appeared beneath the team name, with a short paragraph giving family or personal information, such as favorite sports and pastimes. Photographs of recent events were also displayed: the commissioning of a new machine, a party to celebrate a quality milestone, or a family picnic in the Rocky Mountains.

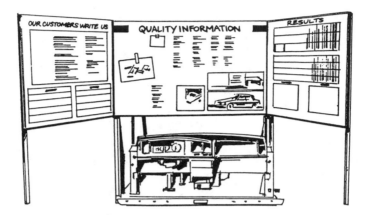

Figure 2-12. J. Reydel plant, Gondecourt, France. Display stand showing products as they are installed by clients. In the right and left panels, quality indicators are reported graphically

This personalizing approach can be applied to any industry. Why should people in offices have their names on their doors while the workers on the floor remain anonymous? It may not be as easy to personalize a manufacturing area as an office, but with some effort, a solution can always be found. For example, some plants have found that the problem of employee mobility can be solved easily by attaching the photographs to magnetic cards that employees take with them when they go to work in other sections.

Defining Roles

In a plant that has adopted team-based organization, the same basic group may have frequent changes of work locations. Everyone is able to operate different machines, handle quality control functions, perform administrative and technical tasks, and participate in working groups. In some American plants, the team leader uses a floor plan to arrange magnetic cards with photographs of each team member according to their responsibilities on a given day. (Figure 2-13) Like a diagram of football players on the field, it shows who is playing in each position. Roles are clearly defined, and when members are away from their usual locations, others know immediately where to find them.

This type of two-dimensional depiction also possesses a symbolic meaning. Whereas the lists encountered in plants are usually enumerations, a chart shows that each individual is

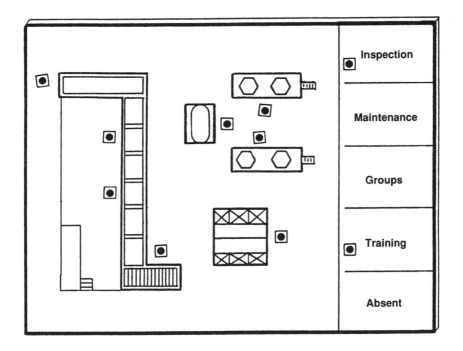

■ = photographs on magnetic cards

Figure 2-13. A personnel distribution chart showing the location of team members on a given day.

defined in terms of relationships with others and has the ability
to change locations, to communicate, to observe, and to provide assistance. Two-dimensional portrayal reinforces not only
group cohesion, but also the objective of becoming more mobile and versatile.

Managing and Organizing the Work Force

In some companies, additional information about the
team's activities is placed beside the identification chart. For example, one might find a training chart listing the dates of up-
coming sessions, the names of members who are receiving
training, and opinions on previous sessions. In some instances,
a chart indicating team members' levels of training is mounted
beside this chart. (Figure 6-5)

Other information that can be displayed includes a schedule indicating team meetings for forthcoming weeks or information concerning other group events. Some plants also post work
force schedules, which simultaneously allow planning of time
away from work and record work attendance. Examples of
these schedules are shown in Chapter 6.

PROVIDING A COMMUNICATION AREA

By establishing an official communication area, a company
pursues two objectives. The first is to facilitate group work.
Most of the messages pertaining to the team, such as general
information, the status of current projects, or performance indicators can be available in one location. A more detailed analysis of the preparation of this type of panel is found in Chapters
6 and 7.

Second, the act of demarcating an explicit communication
area symbolically reinforces the team's new responsibilities for
control. If the company intends to ensure that the team itself

and other members of the company recognize these responsibilities, it should not hesitate to emphasize visual indications.

When for the first time a company organizes meetings such as quality circles for machine operators, it often holds them in a room in the office area. If the plant is not extremely compact, however, participants in these meetings must go to an unfamiliar section of the plant that is far from their usual workplaces. This situation is also impractical: Necessary documents and information are elsewhere, and it is difficult for workers to return quickly to their workplaces to examine concrete circumstances or to pose questions to someone not at the meeting.

It is preferable, therefore, to provide a meeting place within a given territory or work area. At the Citroën plant in Caen, France, areas within the production section have been marked in red to designate locations for meetings and communications. (Figure 2-14) Brief but frequent meetings occur in these locations; longer meetings are held in a designated room.

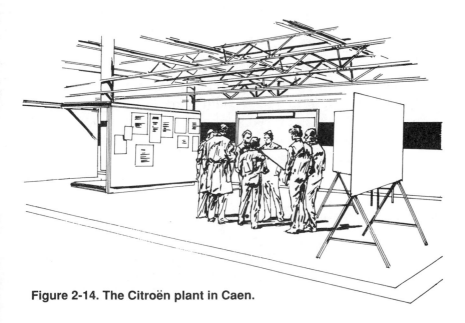

Figure 2-14. The Citroën plant in Caen.

General Information

This heading concerns general plant or company activities, namely information usually posted at entrances to work areas or printed in employee newsletters. This book will not examine the topic of general information in detail. Specialized works on internal communication describe ways to create a company newsletter, conduct surveys, or distribute reports to the entire work force. (See the Bibliography.)

Including general information within a visual organization framework does not present any significant problems. Boards for posting messages are available, as are more effective resources such as electronic illuminated boards, terminals in work areas, and computerized information network terminals, all of which allow real-time transmission of information.

To maintain uniformity with the essential features of visual organization, it is important to uphold two principles:

- Do not convey information without first determining whether it generates interest. Production of information should always be preceded by development of needs. To verify needs, one method is the self-service approach. (See the example below from Fleury Michon.)
- Create an information system that is directly relevant. From the outset everyone must be well informed about the immediate environment. To speak about the company in general is useless if someone is unaware of what is happening in his or her work area.

The Fleury Michon Video Magazine

In Pouzauges, France, the firm of Fleury Michon has adopted a video magazine format that, according to the firm's communication manager, is high successful. Reports Mr. Petit:

A magazine isn't written to satisfy its editorial staff; it's created to interest readers. We measure the audience on a regular basis. Last year, it was 37 percent of workers, and it has risen to 50 percent this year. There's only one way to gain people's interest, namely, to focus closely on their concerns. One of the factors behind the success of our video magazine is that it's produced by a former worker who was deeply interested in photography before he received video training. He finds appropriate language, ideas that take root, and an effective way of presenting topics.

This is a monthly magazine, provided on a self-service basis on a television set located near the changing rooms, in a comfortable area with chairs. Each magazine is approximately 20 minutes long and there are always three segments. One consists of a description of a company department. Another covers the personal interests of the employees, and

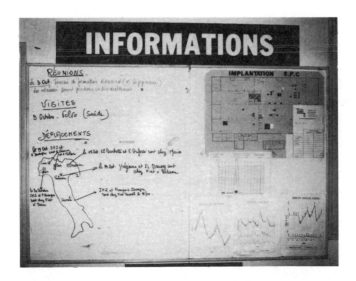

Figure 2-15. The Favi plant at Hallencourt, France. This chart at a plant that manufactures copper alloy items announces forthcoming meetings and customer visits. A map of Italy indicates visits by the firm's sales forces. The plant map in the upper right section identifies machines recently outfitted with process control systems for statistical process control.

they can appear on camera to explain their hobbies. The last segment reports on a general topic associated with the company's activities, or with one of its projects. The narration is provided by a volunteer, who becomes the anchor person for that month.

Down-to-Earth Information

In Quebec, Canada, in the principal work area of the Camoplast plant, which produces plastic components for automobiles, a large illuminated panel hangs from the ceiling. Many cities use these panels to communicate public information to their inhabitants. Many plants have now acquired panels of this kind. At Camoplast, the nature of the messages transmitted is different. In addition to general information, employees see

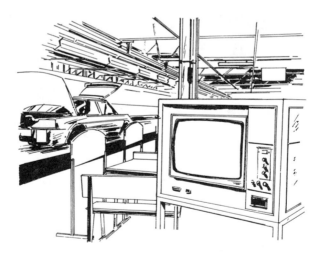

Figure 2-16. The Renault plant at Sandouville. Video monitors in the work area introduce plans for new models and communicate new methods or procedures. A weekly video magazine allows each member of the work force to obtain news about his or her department, as well as information about the rest of the plant.

such announcements as: "The press operating team has reduced the tool-changing period from 32 minutes to 19 minutes," or "Eight days with no downtime on the crankcase line." The company makes a significant effort to transmit directly relevant news.

KEEPING A TERRITORY NEAT AND ORDERLY

This is the story of a miraculously transformed plant. In 1982, General Motors closed its Fremont, California, plant after an accumulation of disastrous performances. In 1984, the plant reopened as New United Motor Manufacturing, Inc. (NUMMI).[5] Over 80 percent of the workers who were rehired had been former GM employees. Today this plant employs 2,800 persons. Various factors led to a spectacular improvement in productivity and quality. The most prominent factors include a Japanese-style just-in-time production system and comprehensive mobilization of the work force to achieve total quality. ("Just-in-time" is a logistical principle describing an organization that functions with minimum inventory levels.)

The NUMMI plant will be mentioned again, because it relies on visual communication to a significant extent (as often happens in plants influenced by the Japanese model). The organization is wholly based on the concept of teamwork. Groups of five to ten members operate in the work areas; the first level of the hierarchy oversees three to five teams.

The large stamping unit area, where presses are situated, is impressive for its neatness and orderliness. Just beyond the entrance an imposing array of brooms is positioned near the first

---

[5] NUMMI is a joint venture established by Toyota Motor Company and General Motors in 1984. The plant produces compact models for the American market, initially the Toyota Corolla FX and Chevrolet Nova, and currently the Toyota Corolla sedan and the Geo Prizm for Chevrolet.

line of presses. Five brooms of varying sizes and shapes are lined up on a brightly colored rack, as if in a parade.

This plant is proud of its technology (one of the most modern lines of stamping presses in the world), but it is no less proud of its housekeeping.

This is a recent phenomenon. Not long ago, a plant bustling with activity, cluttered and disorderly, with crowded aisles where everyone scurried about, was regarded as a prosperous plant. Today, however, ideas have changed. In American plants, housekeeping is mentioned frequently. Great care is given to the premises. Orderliness and neatness now occupy a high rank on the scale of values for plants — on the same level as technology or automation.

Order and neatness are closely related to visual communication. Among visual messages, we first observe the messages conveyed by the objects that surround us. If their messages defy our comprehension, as in the instance of a work area where the positioning of objects is not controlled, part of the communication network disappears. This situation existed at the Fichet Bauche plant with the old method of handling orders.

If a workplace is dirty or chaotic, the environment transmits incomprehensible messages. Why have finished parts been placed in an area for parts that are not ready? Why are tools not returned to their locations after repairs? Why does a container lack an approval label? Like the static in a poor telephone connection, disorder interferes with every level of visual communication.

In every factory where a successful visual mode of organization has been introduced, work areas are remarkably well ordered and clean. Thus, the first step in a visual communication project is to rearrange the work area, repaint the machines, and sweep the floors.

Everyone is aware of neatness. After a plant reorganization involving millions of dollars and years of effort, the first change those who spend their days on the premises see is the cleanliness.

Figure 2-17. A view of the carburetor finishing section at the Solex plant, Evreux, France — an example of industrial housekeeping.

Astute clients, of course, do not allow themselves to be deceived. During plant visits, a glance evaluates management's ability to establish rules, ensure compliance, and be careful with details. If cigarette butts are lying on the floor, the firm's products probably have some defects that seemed unimportant to the person who completed the products.

Fully Allocate Space

Allocating space consists of marking areas and colored lines on the floor, labeling shelves for tool storage, and designating any locations that may be useful for arranging items. Each square meter on the floor, each section, and each position should be intended for a specific use. The principle is simple: A place for everything, and everything in its place.

Proper space allocation and labeling enable the code (colors, photographs, reference marks, storage racks) to become a simple language accessible to everyone and easy to apply. Workers should be able to find and arrange items unassisted, without disrupting the order of the territory. In Chapter 4 we will look at production and inventory flow control methods that are based entirely on floor markings.

The allocation of space demands a rigorous discipline, because it requires anticipation of anything that may occur in the specific territory; if the flow of work-in-process is not under control it is difficult to allocate space accurately. The advantage to this requirement is that once space has been distributed, any item without a place poses a problem requiring immediate resolution. It is impossible to place the item in a corner and pretend that it does not exist. The system creates its own maintenance function.

OPENING PLANTS TO VISITORS

In plants where visitors are rarely allowed to enter work areas or are admitted in such a concealed manner that no one knows who they are, employees are affected by the "empty-

Figure 2-18. Placement of tools near a group of machines at the Solex plant in Evreux.

Figure 2-19. A team's technical area at the Valeo plant near Le Mans.
The assumption of technical responsibilities by production teams is relatively
recent and has not yet become a conventional phenomenon. Technical
departments feel no need to prove that they are responsible for maintaining
machines — the organization chart makes their role visible. If a production
team is also expected to consider itself responsible for this function, however,
the plant must emphasize the symbolic indications of this responsibility.

When a production team receives responsibilities in a technical domain,
even for disassembling a tool, adjusting a machine, or lubricating a certain
mechanism, a technical area should be provided and designated as such.
The size of this area is relatively unimportant. The main thing is to establish
its identity with a color or an innovative layout. All of the items necessary for
the team's technical duties, — tools, documentation, instructions, malfunction
reports and so on — should be stored in this area.

stadium syndrome." This syndrome is a form of discouragement that athletic teams suffer when they play in inaccessible
stadiums. It is rarely enjoyable to perform an activity without
occasionally thinking of spectators. Without an audience people
tend to become discouraged and can forget the purpose of
their activities.

Once a company develops a visual mode of organization, plant visits become significantly more beneficial. Visitors gain a better understanding of what they will see, and employees begin to take pride in their activities.

In places such as the Bull plant in Angers, France, visits are a distinct component of a quality improvement strategy. According to the communication manager:

> It is important for employees, technicians, or engineers to be in contact with visitors. By providing opportunities to describe their activities, by promoting dialogue with computer users, or with suppliers of components, we are able to facilitate contact among the production sector, the market, and the firm's economic environment. These visits reinforce the entire staff's sense of working for demanding clients who are situated within a dynamic market.

Many plants hesitate to proceed in this direction. Nevertheless, the positive effects of opening the work areas should overcome this hesitation: Spectators should enter the stadium.

FOUR RULES TO MAKE PLANT VISITS MORE EFFECTIVE AND PROFITABLE

One: Announce Visits in Advance

It is astonishing to discover that this rule is not applied in certain plants. It appears natural enough; would you allow strangers to wander into your home without informing you beforehand? Provide announcements by means of a board or an illuminated panel that can be erected at the entrance for this purpose ("We welcome Ms. X, from the Y Company"), or by means of notices posted in work areas.

Two: Involve Employees in Explaining the Work Areas

During the many visits I have made to visual factories, a supervisor or a team leader has begun to serve as my guide as soon as I arrived in his or her section. This method requires a certain amount of forethought. It is necessary to instruct the employee who will serve as a guide and to provide appropriate support.

These kinds of arrangements offer many advantages. During the visit, the people who welcome visitors are able to perform other duties as necessary. Moreover, the visitor observes the way in which the plant's employees perceive the firm's projects. Hearing a machine operator or a team leader explain the advantages of zero inventories or the virtues of total quality can provide knowledgeable visitors with a precise indication of the level of industrial culture within a plant.

Three: Facilitate Explanation

The presence of descriptive panels facilitates explanation, not only for occasional visitors, but also for "open house" days.

When the Télémécanique company organized an open house at its Carros plant, responsibility for the project was entrusted to a working group. One member of the group proposed a simple idea:

> Instead of appointing guides, which would mean mobilizing a fair number of people, why not do what they do at fairs? We can put colored strips on the floor, so that people will have a precise path to follow. Then we wait in our work areas, like exhibitors selling their products at booths. Each team can prepare a chart to explain the nature of its activities, how different processes take place, what its projects are, and the results.

Four: Take Advantage of Visitors' Observations

Visitors have a new way of looking at a plant. Their observations, offered with a certain detachment, are often interesting to workers in a plant. The company should not be reluctant to inform employees about visitors' opinions with respect to the organization and operation of various work areas. At the Renault Sandouville plant, every visitor completes a brief questionnaire, noting observations about order and neatness. (Figure 6-7) The results are published in the company newsletter and displayed at the main entrance of the plant.

3

Visual Documentation

Around 1900, Frederick Winslow Taylor began to formulate the basis for a scientific approach to work. Until then, individuals had done their jobs in their own ways. Although factories had small numbers of skilled workers or senior personnel whose know-how had been developed over the years, the majority of the labor force consisted of untrained workers who seldom knew how to perform efficient, high-quality work. During that era, there was little sharing of knowledge, quest for efficiency, or possibility of progress.

Taylor observed the activities of workers who shoveled coal in steel mills in Bethlehem, Pennsylvania. By analyzing the movements of the most efficient workers, determining the optimum size of the shovel for the density of the material to be transferred, and enabling other mills to learn about advances in a given mill, Taylor demonstrated that it was possible to increase efficiency of production without investing in new equipment.

Taylor's innovation was to apply scientific principles to a relatively unexplored field. Increased physical effort, he felt, was fruitless; the required solution was to work more effectively. For work to be performed more effectively in any organization, methods must be developed. Thus, it was necessary to observe and to analyze tasks, to seek ideas, and to experiment and generalize. Taylor's objective was to organize know-how efficiently and to promote sharing of knowledge within individual factories. In this way each company would become more prosperous.

Doubtless, in 1900, many workers lacked sufficient academic knowledge to participate in scientific work analysis as Taylor conceived it. They were not incapable, however, of observing, analyzing, and making suggestions, which Taylor understood. Nevertheless, the era was marked by growth. Companies needed to advance quickly. Unlike today, they did not aim to increase productivity by merely ten or fifteen percent. Often they could achieve twofold, threefold, or even greater savings in time.

Specialization and centralization were the order of the day. Taylor made the analysis of work into a function of the staff, which evolved into the industrial engineering department.

The consequences are familiar. Factories became larger, and were subdivided. Industrial engineering departments became more removed from the floor. A sense of estrangement from formal knowledge slowly began to dominate the factory assembly line. Once the understanding of Taylor's principles was lost, the entire concept of formal methods lost credibility. Administrative departments complained that production units did not respect written directions, and the production units replied that standards were improperly formulated and at times wholly inapplicable. Taylor's dream — to enhance the formalization of methods in order to render organizations more efficient — was superseded by "Taylorism."

STANDARDIZED WORK: THE "ORIGINAL SIN" OF WESTERN INDUSTRY

Japanese production methods — just-in-time, total quality, increased employee participation in decision making — have become familiar in the West. While these methods run counter to the habits of most Western factories, they are widely recognized as necessary to restore industrial competitiveness.

Shigeo Shingo is regarded as one of the world's leading exponents of these methods. In the introduction to a 1985 book, Shingo wrote:

> In 1931, I ran across a translation of Taylor's book [*The Principles of Scientific Management* (New York: Harper & Brothers, 1911)] in a neighborhood bookstore. Thumbing through it, I found a most unusual statement. "Inexpensive goods," it said, "can be produced even when workers are paid high wages." The apparent impossibility of such a proposition aroused my suspicions, and as I continued to leaf through the book, I saw that Taylor claimed the feat was possible if efficiency was raised to a high level.
>
> For me, this argument was utterly novel, so I bought the book and did not sleep until I had read it from cover to cover. At that point I resolved to devote my life to scientific management. . . .
>
> . . . My thinking is based on Frederick Taylor's analytical philosophy, and under Professor [Ken'ichi] Horikome's tutelage has been deeply colored by Frank Gilbreth's exhaustive pursuit of goals and the single best method. Indeed, this has been the basic thrust of my own industrial engineering improvement courses.[1]

Shingo is not the only admirer of Taylor and his standard methods. Katsuyoshi Ishihara, one of Japan's leading quality specialists, writes: "Manufacturing good products is possible only if workers rigorously abide by operating standards. An operating standard is a document indicating the proper way to proceed so as to achieve quality. It is not possible to manufacture

---

[1] Shigeo Shingo, *The Sayings of Shingo – Key Strategies for Plant Improvement*, (Cambridge, MA: Productivity Press, 1985), pp. xv-xvii.

good products without respecting standards or by letting everyone work according to his own notions."[2]

Kiyoshi Suzaki compares production to an orchestra. In his opinion, synchronization of various work stations is like the rhythm achieved by musicians. The quality of a given procedure is like the tone of an instrument, and coordination among various locations within a work area can be compared to an orchestra's overall harmony. "Only when these elements are in place," he says, "can an orchestra play beautiful music. Standard work in the factory is similar to the music score for each musician. In our factories, standard work is a tool to achieve maximum performance with minimum waste."[3]

Conversely, in the West, Taylor's ideas have acquired such an unfavorable reputation that people hesitate to say whether the act of writing precise instructions is itself beneficial or harmful. A question from the audience after a lecture in which I upheld the principle of detailed displaying of instruction is evidence of this irony: "Doesn't this exceptional accuracy that you value so much clash with the autonomy that you have also stated is one of the principles of modern management?"

A fundamental misunderstanding exists because the formalization of methods is regarded as an obstacle to autonomy, as if being "autonomous" requires people to avoid following explicit instructions or respecting precise rules. The collectively oriented culture of the Japanese enables them to value formal methods for their virtues of communication and progress, rather than for authority.

---

[2] Katsuyoshi Ishihara, *Manuel pratique de gestion de la qualité* (Paris: Editions de l'A.F.N.O.R., 1986).

[3] Kiyoshi Suzaki, *The New Manufacturing Challenge* (New York: Free Press, 1987), p. 136.

A TABOO: EMPLOYEE DEVELOPMENT
OF WORK INSTRUCTIONS

Workers themselves can develop the work instructions in cooperation with technical departments. This idea did not enter the mind of my questioner in the previous anecdote because our industrial culture is dominated by numerous prejudices.

Many companies find it difficult to allow production personnel to participate in the domain of creating instructions. Consider the following situation reported in a journal article:

> Inspired by the difficulties that existed in terms of operating the system, an employee in a flexible production unit took the initiative of preparing an operating manual explaining all of the steps that he performed to overcome malfunctions. This extremely well-prepared document was often used by his co-workers. Nevertheless, the reaction of his superiors was complete indifference, and the worker became deeply embittered as a result.[4]

The authors concluded by observing that it was unlikely this worker would ever again become involved in the functioning of his workplace to this degree.

In the minds of many, writing is reserved for administrative personnel, even though in this era the majority of production workers have been educated. Another assumption is that creating rules, explaining methods, or issuing instructions are privileges of departments outside the factory floor; these managers are the only ones who can make the law.

Visual communication comes into dramatic conflict with this archaic taboo. Production teams should not only be asked to participate in developing ranges of tolerance, instructions,

---

4 Article by Michel Berry based on research by A. Rosanvallon and J.-F. Troussier, *Annales des mines*, January, 1988.

and other visual directions, but their activities should become a strategic device for increasing efficiency. Production teams can offer knowledge at the precise location of a given process to control know-how more effectively.

Should Taylor be reconsidered? People can read his works and decide for themselves. Westerners, however, who assign him blame for most of the problems affecting industry commit an error. They have been confused between the tools and the method of using them, or between the essential concept of formal knowledge and the authority certain departments derive from it. By criticizing Taylor, they have blamed the tools, whereas the problem is the redefinition of the roles of the people using these tools.

The Team and the Chronometer

On a visit to the NUMMI plant in Fremont, California, I was amazed by the number, variety, and precision of the visual documentations of work methods and instructions. Among the visual aids near the assembly line, I encountered work- and time-study diagrams of the type Gilbreth invented at the beginning of the twentieth century.

William Borton, the manager of the stamping plant (now assistant general manager for production control), feels that these documents were not innovative. What is unusual about them, however, is that assembly-line personnel perform the analyses. A working group of machine operators is responsible for analyzing time and motion. These operators clock one another. The chronometric results enable the group to understand how its most efficient members work. When an improvement is introduced, the documentation is updated. "The frequency of these updates is the best indicator of workers' ability to pursue initiatives," according to Borton.

A KNOWLEDGE FIELD

In Taylor's crusade for the scientific organization of work, he launched a long process of codification of knowledge. Technical documentation (tolerances, work instructions, operating instructions for machinery, and so on) concretely represents this transformation of employees' knowledge into centralized knowledge. (Figure 3-1) When control of this codification process becomes a component of authority, however, the system degenerates. Production units lose the ability to pursue initiatives, and administrative departments regain this authority.

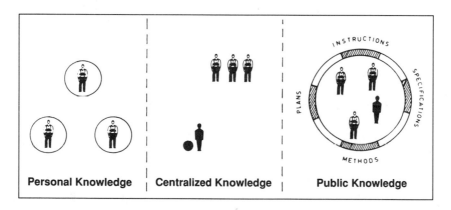

Figure 3-1. The role of visual documentation: converting the workplace into a knowledge field.

Every company should ask itself persistently until a practical answer emerges, "Why must knowledge be a sign of authority within an organization?" Why do individuals persist in hoarding knowledge to the detriment of the group, when the only reasonable objective is sharing knowledge to achieve synergy and allow a company to become stronger?

Visual organization characteristically offers a concrete response to these questions. The act of displaying documentation dramatically changes the manner in which this conflict of authority ensues.

Indeed, when documents become accessible (that is, visible and understandable) where activities occur, when knowing is systematically followed by communicating knowledge, where information appears in public spaces, and where the manufacturing landscape is transformed into a true visual data base, the problem of possession of knowledge can be approached differently.

A dramatic transformation can occur, resembling a Copernican revolution. With visual organization, knowledge no longer belongs to Peter, or to Paula, or to a specialist, or to the supervisor of Peter and Paula. Knowledge no longer belongs to any individual. People now belong to a knowledge field.

A CONTEMPORARY TREATISE ON METHOD

The Solex plant in Evreux, France, manufactures carburetors for automobiles. Until recently, quality control was entrusted to a specialized department. This approach is the root of multiple problems — eliminating defects at their source is more difficult, and production flows are slower. These factors induced the plant's managers to introduce self-inspection. Workers have become responsible for the quality of the carburetors they assemble, and they inspect the product directly.

To fulfill these additional responsibilities under suitable conditions, Solex's technical specialists developed extremely rigorous work and inspection methods. They prepared sheets of instructions, vital information about quality, and inspection rules. These sheets are placed near each machine, in rotary holders that are accessible at all times. (Figure 3-2)

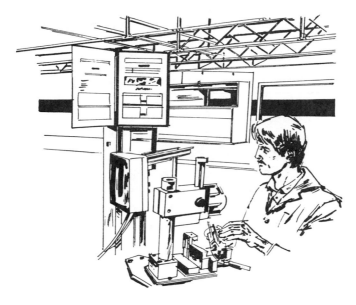

Figure 3-2. The Solex plant in Evreux. Sheets containing instructions are always available at work stations (see detail in Figure 3-14).

Our Bible

One worker who assembled carburetors said, "We used to be timid about bothering our foreman with details or minor doubts, and that often led to mistakes."

By citing a lower likelihood of errors as an advantage of detailed instruction sheets, the Solex workers confirmed an obvious result. "One thing impressed me a lot," said one worker. "During the training program, we were told that even if the company's general manager were to stand beside someone and ask him to change an instruction sheet or to use methods that were different from the indicated method, we could refuse. We would be able to say, 'I'm sorry, sir, but that sheet defines our procedures, and that's how we do our work. Nothing on the sheet can be changed until the entire shop approves it.'" This worker also said, "Now we constantly rely on what's written down. The instruction sheets and the inspection sheets are our Bible."

The adaptation process has worked perfectly. The issue of whether relying on the directions on the sheets reflects a dependency on an external department is gone. Rather, the users regard the documents as tools for becoming more independent.

No longer do workers need to determine whether instructions express the industrial engineering department's ideas or the managers' wishes. The sheets represent an objective concept of the proper way to perform work, a concept that has been approved by the users and will be constantly tested against reality.

Visual documentation comprises a contemporary treatise on method. It is hard to overstate the profound importance of this change: By a reversal of perspective — by proceeding from imposed standardization to shared standardization — the concept of standard methods has regained its good reputation.

Success with this process depends on the way the preparatory phase is handled. Initiating a visual documentation project at the location where the use will occur is easy. Ensuring employees' participation is more difficult.

Before self-inspection was introduced, the Solex workers received fifteen hours of training in which the role of written instructions was fully explained. Documents were carefully designed and a system to allow prompt updating was developed. (Figure 3-15)

The entire staff — shop-level supervisory personnel and specialized technical departments — participates in the process. When projects that aim to significantly change relationships between people and knowledge are launched, the entire company environment must be transformed.

A ROAD MAP

Physio-Control is a leading American manufacturer of electronic medical equipment, notably cardiac defibrillators. Entering the firm's ultra-modern plant on the outskirts of Seattle, Washington, one can understand what constitutes a visual facility. There are spotlessly clean work areas, bright colors, and living green plants. Several communication and rest areas are arranged in a homely manner at various locations. Wherever one looks, forms of communication command attention: identification of activities, production charts near the assembly lines, boards where employees can record problems occurring on a given day, and so on.

Approaching the work stations, one encounters rotary panels with visual material for the work stations, including instruction sheets and color diagrams. "These sheets haven't been here very long," said a production manager.

> They were put here during the period when we had started working on a just-in-time basis. Until then, we had not encountered any serious assembly problems, just ordinary occurrences for any plant. Difficulties arose when we attempted to reduce inventories. At that point it became necessary to work with small production runs and to change employees' work locations frequently, to meet market demand more reliably. Then we encountered a proliferation of minor errors that led to a steady increase in the level of rejections during inspections.

Unsuitable Documents

"We already had technical instructions," the manager continued, "but they were not displayed at the work stations."

The day we decided to create documents that would be much easier to read, to give our employees more autonomy, the industrial engineer established a research group. The idea was that workers would be asked to indicate the instructions that they hoped would be available, and to indicate the format that they considered most appropriate.

We discovered that the coordinating engineer for the work group had himself prepared the original sheets. He honestly believed that they were good. During the discussions, he was astonished to learn that the texts of the official documents were generally unsuitable. They lacked clarity and in some instances were ambiguous.

At that point I became aware of a significant fact: The line manager was spending most of his time explaining how the workers should do their jobs. As a result, he was neglecting his managing and organizing functions. Of course, this situation was the source of additional difficulties.

If we understand the production manager correctly, under the earlier system work documents probably existed in the form of an official version and an "actually used" version. This distortion obliged the line manager to function constantly as an intermediary between the engineering department and the workers. The more often the workers had to change work stations or procedures, the more the line manager was overwhelmed and the less attention he could give to technical matters and coordination. His duties had been transformed. He had gradually become an unwilling intermediary for defective communication.

The absence of appropriate documentation does not necessarily produce problems with quality or reduce efficiency. This aspect is deceptive, however. Things may proceed satisfactorily for years, until the point when the firm may be confronted by unstable markets that force it to reduce production periods and inventories.

At this point, the absence of a system of direct information becomes cruelly apparent. While a worker who repeats the same procedure for an extended period may dispense with written instructions, one who occupies a work station for only a few hours must be able to consult unambiguous instructions. Otherwise, the quality of work suffers.

This is why in firms that want to be simultaneously flexible and productive, access to knowledge should be immediate — literally, without intermediaries. Then supervisory personnel can pursue their true roles: guiding, organizing, and planning.

The Third Component of Flexibility

Flexibility includes several components. The first two — those that come to mind most frequently — are the selection of physical resources (multipurpose machinery, rapid changing of tools) and personnel-management policies (part-time workers, variable schedules).

The third component of flexibility, however, is an increase in mobility of physical resources. Such mobility depends on better communication within the entire environment: machinery, means of storage, maintenance resources, tools, information systems, and administrative systems.

To summarize the concept with an image: In knowledge fields, everyone should possess the necessary maps to find the way without a guide.

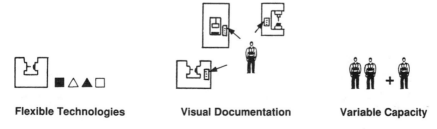

Flexible Technologies   **Visual Documentation**   **Variable Capacity**

Figure 3-3. The three components of flexibility.

A STARTING POINT TO ACHIEVE PROGRESS

Prejudices are tenacious. Two prejudices about factories have survived for a long time. The first proclaims that standard documents are the concern of the offices, not the shop floor. The basis of visual documentation is to affirm the opposite. Everyone, especially production units, should be involved with the creation of standard documents.

The second prejudice declares that standards are created to last. With the premise that a specialized department has developed standards, the stability of a standard is seen as a sign of its quality. The consequences of such a stultifying concept of how to develop standards are disastrous.

Visual organization, once again, reverses the principle. A good standard constantly evolves. The expression is somewhat paradoxical, but it conveys the idea that, in the new approach to methods, the role of standards has changed. Standards are no longer solely intended to define methods: Their role is to inspire improvements.

The visibility of documents will play an extremely precise role in the constant questioning of standards. Because they are accessible to everyone, standard documents will be permanently subject to criticism and suggestions for improvement (indeed, frequent changing of work stations will increase such comments).

If the instructions say "Pick up the sheets in groups of three," and a member of the team considers it possible to place four sheets under the press once the edges have been trimmed, then she can propose modification of the standard. If the instructions say, "Allow two exposures to the preheating tunnel," and an operator observes that a single exposure is sufficient on the maximum temperature setting, then he can propose a modification of that standard.

Abundant motivation exists. If a user's efforts succeed, and the new method is accepted by the group, he or she contributes to the development of an official document for the company. Displaying standards is a way of acknowledging the responsibilities and accomplishments of those who contribute to them.

The role of visual documentation therefore clearly emerges. Introducing a document into shared space — submitting it to a process of public scrutiny — results in better ownership of the knowledge and opportunities for constructive criticism.

These opportunities arise even more frequently according to how precise documents are. Thus, precision, which was seen as lack of freedom when documents were prepared outside the group, becomes a component of progress when updating is in the hands of the users. The circular dynamic of developing standards can be understood properly: A standard is a point of reference that simultaneously provides the group with a point to adhere to and a point of departure.

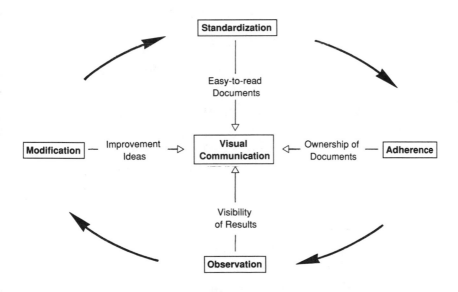

Figure 3-4. Standards are needed to turn the wheel of progress.
Visual organization facilitates the entire process.

SUMMARY

After a century in which the power struggle within the workplace has revolved around control of knowledge, new forms of communication are introducing a profound transformation of the relationship between human beings and knowledge. We can summarize this transformation in three points:

1. The users become directly involved in managing knowledge and developing their own methods.
2. Visual documentation in a work location creates a knowledge field, where the sharing of information and adaptation of rules and methods will occur.
3. Visual communication offers two advantages:
   - The employees' autonomy and mobility are enhanced, thereby facilitating achievement of quality while also reducing some unproductive mediation functions for supervisory personnel.
   - The visibility of standards becomes a decisive factor in employees' participation in ongoing progress.

STAGES OF DEVELOPING VISUAL DOCUMENTATION

A company that pursues visual presentation of knowledge must complete certain stages, and respect certain rules. Next I will analyze the practical aspects of that process in four principal phases:

- Defining the field covered
- Selecting the media
- Establishing a system that allows rapid updating
- Promoting employee participation

Defining the Field Covered

This task is the starting point for a visual documentation project. The etymology of the word "document" is "to teach." Hence, visual documentation fulfills two roles: to transmit knowledge and to provide instructions. This interpretation is purposely extremely general. A company that decides to adopt visual documentation has a vital interest in viewing the project in the broadest possible terms from the beginning.

This expansion of perspective occurs along two axes: One axis defines sectors of the plant that will participate in the project, and the other the nature of the topics being covered.

Expansion to Other Sectors

In addition to a technique, visual documentation is an approach. If the approach is valid, why shouldn't it be applied in every sector of a plant that could benefit from it?

If displaying methods and knowledge is useful in production units, why not — in suitable form — use it in technical departments, offices, or warehouses? If introducing knowledge to a public domain helps prevent errors, increases flexibility in organizing work, and creates favorable conditions for improvement, why reserve this approach solely for production teams?

A firm that encourages all of its departments to participate in scrutinizing visual documentation increases the likelihood of success. A general process begins, with a dynamic that affects the entire plant. The firm also clearly affirms that rather than reinforcing rules to control the workers, this project is intended to produce a highly significant transformation of relationships between individuals and collective knowledge.

In other words, broadening the principle of displaying knowledge to include other sectors of a plant is a way of affirming the cultural scope of the project, beyond the merely technical elements. We will discuss this idea again in relation to other applications of visual communication.

Expansion of Topics

When the aim of visual documentation ceases to be the imposition of external constraints or control and becomes a promotion of sharing, attitudes change. A change of perspective occurs toward the development of standard methods.

Whereas with the traditional approach it was necessary to emphasize presentation of concepts that people do not know in black and white, now everyone must think about the written expression of known concepts, so that others may benefit.

Hence, anything that a few people know should be visibly expressed, if such knowledge might facilitate the activities of a wider group. Any information or instructions that might allow clearer understanding of work at any level is relevant to the new approach to sharing knowledge.

With this viewpoint, visual documentation acquires new expressions: photographs with red dots indicating possible malfunctions (Figure 3-5), a positioning grid drawn on the floor, an array of parts alongside their respective codes (Figure 3-13), or a series of colored markings indicating locations for inspecting oil levels in a machine. (Figure 3-10)

This visual expansion offers two advantages. First, a portion of the documents can be generated by the workers. Communication surpasses traditional written media, and becomes more accessible by using peripheral resources: Instant photographs and felt-tipped pens are often more effective than typewriters for the workers at a given production location.

The other advantage is symbolic. By expanding the range of visual documentation, a firm launches a collective endeavor in which each person can participate at his or her own level. A machinist who proposes use of colored markings on a set of instructions to avoid reversing two procedures does nothing

risk sheet

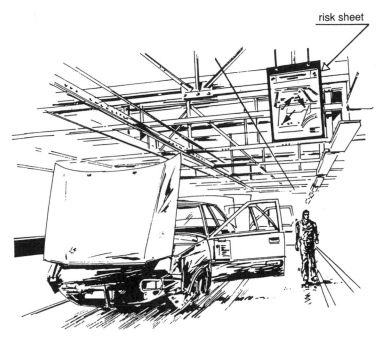

Figure 3-5. The Renault plant in Sandouville. "Risk sheets" hanging over the line use colored indicators to note critical points in various procedures.

different than a technician who uses computer-aided design to define an optimum machining range on a digitally controlled machine. At their own levels, each of them is developing the company's official know-how.

Examples of Visual Information in a Workplace

1. Methods and organization
   - Manufacturing tolerances and instruction sheets for various procedures
   - Time-motion studies, planning of work
   - Self-inspection instructions, sheets indicating risks
   - Auditing procedures

- Recommendations concerning quality and identification of critical points in operating procedures
- Marking of surfaces
- Balancing of work stations
- Storage and identification of semi-finished items
- Inventory levels in the vicinity of work stations, or in warehouses
- Other standards and rules for operations control
- Procedures, rules, safety and health

2. Resources and technology
   - Operating instructions for equipment
   - Replacement and adjustment of tools
   - Maintenance and troubleshooting procedures
   - Monitoring and servicing procedures
   - Description of processes and technologies
   - General manufacturing procedures
   - Plant layout and flow charts

3. Products and materials
   - Product specifications
   - Required materials and components
   - Parts lists
   - Packaging requirements
   - Identification of common defects in materials and products

Selecting Media

Bendix Electronics, a company employing 800 people at its plant in Toulouse, France, produces electronic items for automobiles (lighting and brake-system components, for instance). In seeking to maintain the quality levels of its output, the firm developed a highly coherent set of diagrams for work stations. (Figures 3-6 and 3-7) The diagrams served as instruction sheets, while also showing maintenance procedures for machinery, and directions for starting and monitoring specific machines.

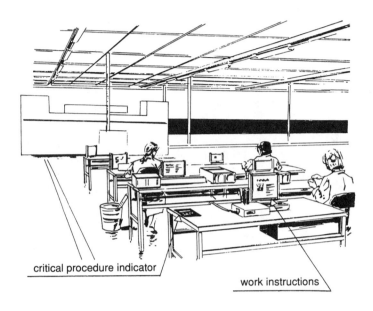

critical procedure indicator

work instructions

Figure 3-6. The Bendix plant in Toulouse. Because there are too many documents to place beside the work stations, vertical U-shaped holders have been installed to hold the instruction sheets between transparent plates. Bright yellow signs on the left corners of some tables indicate that the procedure is critical to the final quality of the product. This type of indicator is an interesting example of visual documentation. The sign is clearly visible and its presence helps employees remember not to skip any instruction sheets.

The visual documentation manager says, "When we started this project, we really didn't believe it would involve so much work." The project consists of itemizing every portion of a firm's methods and knowledge, providing updates in a systematic manner, and organizing dissemination of that information. Nevertheless, the resulting benefits for production make these projects among the best investments that a firm can make.

Clear Information for a Non-specific Audience

At Bendix, a specialist specifically assigned to the manufacturing division prepares all the diagrams for work stations.

Preparing Adhesive Guns

1. Emptying and Cleaning

plunger
gun

bolt

needle

isopropyl alcohol

Clean the 4 elements of the gun.

No traces of adhesive should remain.

- **Clean inside of needle with a suitable bit from the magazine.**

bit

2. Filling the Guns

- **Insert the plastic stopper.**
- **Secure it with a bolt**

stopper

- **Put two guns on the stand.**
- **Fill them with adhesive to 1/3 the total length.**

adhesive

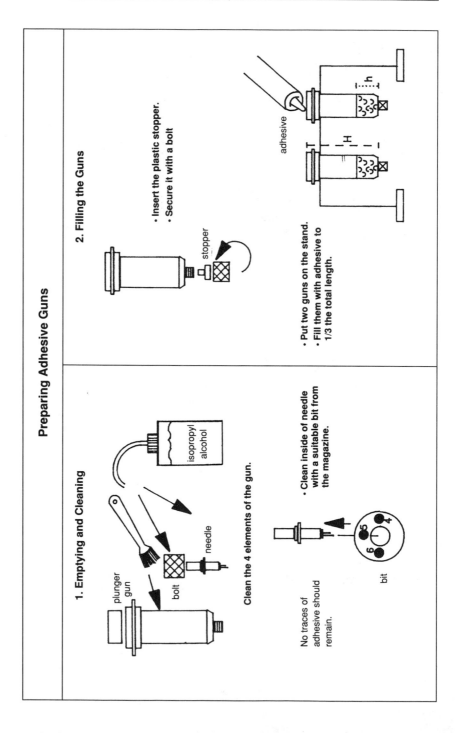

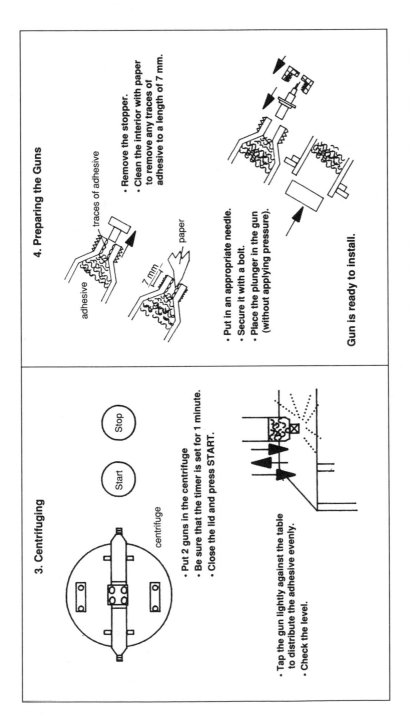

4. Preparing the Guns

adhesive   traces of adhesive

7 mm   paper

- Remove the stopper.
- Clean the interior with paper to remove any traces of adhesive to a length of 7 mm.

- Put in an appropriate needle.
- Secure it with a bolt.
- Place the plunger in the gun (without applying pressure).

Gun is ready to install.

3. Centrifuging

Stop

Start

centrifuge

- Put 2 guns in the centrifuge
- Be sure that the timer is set for 1 minute.
- Close the lid and press START.

- Tap the gun lightly against the table to distribute the adhesive evenly.
- Check the level.

Figure 3-7. The Bendix plant in Toulouse, France. All visual materials for work stations are prepared on a minicomputer, with explanatory diagrams or photographs. Colors are added by hand to emphasize certain points.

The specialist's time is allocated to preparing documents and training employees. With practical experience, the specialist possesses a precise idea of how documents should be prepared:

> The essence of visual documentation is that it should be self-sufficient for an unspecifically defined audience. We should not be satisfied with writing down anything that seems appropriate. We should especially concern ourselves with what users — at least, most users — need. For a document to fulfill its supporting role at all times, many persons must understand it in the same way. When a message provides information for a supervisor, it is understood in a different way than when it is intended to be read by an entire production unit.

In verbal communication, everyone adapts their messages to specific situations. One knows the listener and takes the listener into account in one's mode of expression. It is always possible to clarify certain points if a message is misunderstood.

None of this is possible with visual documentation. Because messages are intended for an audience, they must be perfectly understood by everyone from the beginning.

Another factor makes it difficult to design documents. When visual documentation is being developed, employees come to rely on this written material. They trust the displayed information. The slightest insufficiency or ambiguity in messages, however, may lead to errors.

The preparation of visual documentation, therefore, requires an extremely detailed and thorough approach. It is necessary not only to explain the steps that must be completed but also to consider anything that may be misinterpreted or improperly done. If the text indicates "Fasten the component with bolts," for example, specify the tool to be used as well as the proper tightening pressure. In writing "Close the cover," remember to warn that the machine cannot start again if its cover is placed in an inverted position.

Whereas traditionally technical documents have been intended to promote limited storage and dissemination of knowledge in factories, today workplace documentation must be considered in terms of mass communication. Neither engineers nor technical specialists have been prepared for this task and it is still not included in their training. A learning process is therefore necessary on the job.

Advantages of Communicating with Images

Visual communication must be precise and thorough at the same time, and yet simple. Graphic or photographic resources are valuable for meeting this challenge. Whenever possible, create symbols or use colors rather than composing a lengthy text.

Instant camera snapshots to accompany a text or to highlight critical locations on items are extremely helpful. Videotaping is also a useful way to provide training for certain procedures.

Some firms use films for training. New employees view videotapes before they begin. They can see how experienced personnel operate, which errors should be avoided, the consequences of errors, and vital locations to monitor.

Examples from Ordinary Experiences

In cities or on highways, messages are designed to be interpreted quickly by large numbers of people with little risk of error. The use of symbols (on signs indicating "Danger," "Stop," "Right Turn") offers multiple advantages. Symbols take less time to read. With a limited number of symbols, reading is merely a form of selection.

Symbols enhance mobility. The rules of the road, for instance, enable people to drive automobiles in countries around the world.

Figure 3-8. The J. Reydel plant in Gondecourt. A systematic effort is made to display work instructions. Depending on the nature of various documents, the employees are partially or wholly responsible for producing them. "The advantages of displaying instructions are often immediate in terms of improving quality," according to the production manager.

After the large instruction chart of photographs of critical locations was put up, the rate of defective procedures at the work station declined by 40 percent. Another advantage: displaying the methods allows assembly workers to understand the functions performed by workers in the hot-forming section. Communication within the production unit has improved significantly. (The poster on the right says, "Declare War on Waste!")

Last, the right side of the brain — where images are recognized — functions more rapidly and is capable of establishing correlations more easily than the left side. The right brain stores significant information effectively because it registers information in context.

To produce visual documentation, we can borrow from instructions for products sold to the general public, provided that we adopt properly designed models.

One example of proper communication for non-specialists exists in the field of microcomputers. One factor behind the success of Apple® computers is the company's effort to achieve

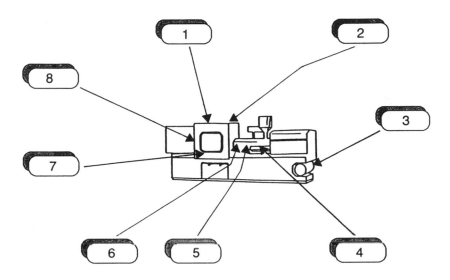

No.	Instructions
1	Check safety devices on tools.
2	Check locking pressure.
3	Check storage cells.
4	Set the temperature.
5	Check clamps.
6	Check probes.
7	Check functioning of end-of-stroke mechanisms.
8	Check functioning of safety devices and alarms.

Figure 3-9. Sample maintenance check sheet. References indicate locations on the machine where the procedure should be performed.

user-friendliness. Instructions that are self-explanatory aid learning; moreover, careless errors rarely produce serious consequences. Many features prevent users from committing errors or help extricate them from difficult situations. Certain programs are excellent examples of mistake-proof systems.

Plant Equipment Is Like a Rental Car

Before driving an automobile for the first time, each of us took lessons, and now we are at ease driving our own cars. Suppose, however, that we rented a car and were unpleasantly surprised to find that there were no indicators for the windshield wipers or the headlights. Suppose that opening the trunk or adjusting the seat position were such complex procedures that we would have to summon the manager to explain the required steps. Clearly, such a lack of user-friendliness would be a serious difficulty in a rental vehicle.

Likewise, in a factory production area, visual documentation should help users commit fewer errors and need assistance less frequently.

Not Just Expression on Paper

If people were restricted to conveying knowledge in the traditional way — on paper — the workplace would quickly resemble the Library of Congress. Especially for information that does not need frequent updating, it is often easier to directly integrate indicators with items of equipment (Figure 3-11) such as symbols attached to a machine. This integration can save time and reduce the likelihood of errors.

Never select media without first understanding the way the user perceives the communication problem. Go to the specific location and consult the people who work there. Often, discussing the situation while standing next to the machine in question will help develop markings that are more economical and more efficient than planning symbols based on the written memoranda generated in someone's office.

Place Information Near Where It Will Be Used

Selecting the location for a visual message is fundamental. Keep in mind that the goals of visual communication are to aid those who use machinery, to save time, and to reduce the likelihood of mistakes.

This principle is recognized in daily experience. If we need to operate a compact disc player but are not entirely familiar with it, having explanations placed directly under the control buttons will make our task easier. The same principle applies in factories. Users who do not have specialized knowledge about a given machine should be able to find all of the necessary information in their immediate surroundings.

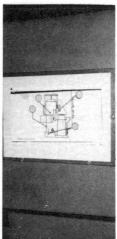

Figure 3-10. The Facom plant in Nevers, France. Colored markings on the machines indicate locations for monitoring oil levels. Each color appearing on the diagram and on the machine corresponds to a different inspection schedule.

Learning is facilitated by placing messages near the location for a given activity. To understand instructions, it is sometimes sufficient to watch another person perform a procedure. By comparing that person's actions with those on the instruction sheet, one can learn twice as quickly as from classroom explanations.[5]

The need for proximity means tailoring appropriate solutions for each situation. Information often must be organized hierarchically, keeping permanent or important information at the work station or near the machine (Figure 3-11), and storing other information nearby. Detailed information that is seldom consulted can be stored at another location in a team's territory.

Advantages for Hands-on Training

NUMMI's William Borton is enthusiastic about hands-on training. In his opinion, cross-training is especially effective when clear information is displayed in the appropriate location:

> In the past, when a new member joined the team, the supervisor had to assume personal responsibility for training. Usually, this training was insufficient because of a lack of time. If someone else were to assume responsibility, however, there was a risk of incomplete or improperly communicated instructions. When a document beside the work station can be used as an aid, various persons can provide training, without sacrificing coherence of explanations.

---

[5] Even with unfamiliar traffic symbols a stranger can quickly adapt in a new city by observing other people's behavior. A New Yorker arriving in Paris would not wait 15 minutes for a "Walk" sign to flash before crossing the street.

Figure 3-11. The Valeo plant near Le Mans. Display of operating instructions on a control panel. The photographs show positions of the robot that may require a specific type of intervention.

Implementing a System for Rapid Updating

Success with a workplace documentation system requires rapid updating. Incorrect or obsolete documents threaten to undermine employee confidence in the entire system.

Approach the updating procedure even more carefully when frequent changes are made because of the level of detail in the documents and suggestions for improvements that the user group may submit.

Figure 3-12. The Solex plant in Evreux. Instruction sheets for preparing cutting tools for a finishing center. This area is situated a few meters from the machine. (The manufacturer of the machine has preadjusted its own cutting tools.)

It is not enough, however, to say, "Do it fast." Rather, build an entire structure that is capable of ensuring rapid updating, regardless of the circumstances. Each aspect must be defined in detail. Who is responsible for updates? What is the procedure, and at what intervals will updates be provided?

If updating is performed by someone outside the group, this person must maintain a close relationship with the unit. This person must make a commitment to complete the updates within a specified time limit.

Promoting Employee Participation

We tried everything. The supervisor called several meetings. We provided training for the entire staff, and we

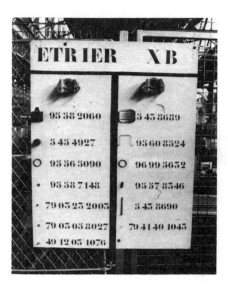

Figure 3-13. The Citroën plant in Caen. Parts are displayed with their reference codes at the entrance to a storage area. Being able to recognize parts is indispensable when inventories are organized on a self-service basis.

explained why it was important to follow rules about health and cleanliness. Large colored posters were put up at the entrance to the work area, but they didn't accomplish anything. It was a failure down the line. In the end, there was only one remedy left, to impose penalties, but that isn't consistent with our usual approach.

How many times have we heard this lament? The inability to obtain compliance with rules occurs frequently and quickly produces conflicts. Within such a context, what can even the most beautiful posters accomplish?

The Fleury Michon company adopted a completely different approach to overcome this situation in the production of prepackaged meat and cooked food. Instead of imposing rules in an authoritarian manner, the firm asked its production workers, with assistance from the quality department, to

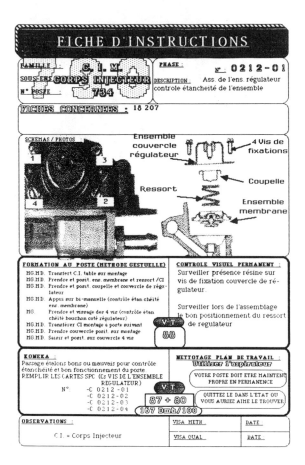

Figure 3-14. Computer-generated documentation at the Solex plant in Evreux. Showing instructions for operations on an injector assembly. Many changes in operating procedures are introduced through workers' efforts. When they recognize safer and more efficient ways of working, they suggest changes in the instruction sheet to their team leaders. If a given change is considered valid, the text is immediately inserted on the current sheet. A duplicate is sent to the appropriate technical specialist as soon as possible.

This person is exclusively responsible for updating instructions, with an office only a few feet from the work area. Within half a day, an updated document will be ready. The quest for efficiency has led Solex to use a computer system combined with a scanning camera to generate these documents (see Figure 3-15).

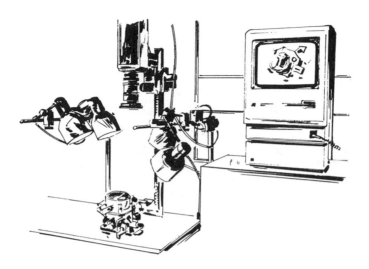

Figure 3-15. Imaging equipment used at the Solex plant in Evreux.
A camera and microcomputer that reproduce an image of a carburetor or component on the instruction sheet. Using a microcomputer data base, it is possible to create a new instruction sheet in an hour, or to introduce updates in 10 minutes. More than 1,000 instruction sheets are in use.

define the rules that should be followed to ensure maximum hygiene in work areas. A working group was established to define appropriate procedures and create a communication panel. (Figure 3-16)

The panel, organized like a comic strip, is visible at the entrance to the production area. Because it depicts procedures defined by the employees, the panel is the group's internal code. Procedures are clearly indicated and every newcomer accepts them.

Fleury Michon illustrates the change of perspective that occurs when the displaying of instructions becomes the responsibility of the employees. By displaying such information, the traditional relationship is inverted. Instead of displaying something that is not known by the workers on the floor, it is necessary

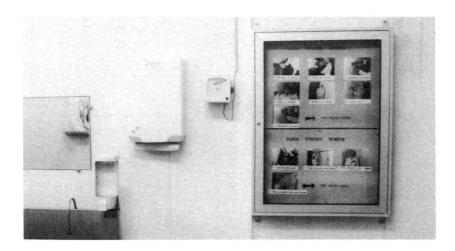

Figure 3-16. Hygiene instructions at the Fleury Michon plant in Pouzages, France. These instructions are displayed at the entrance to an area where hams are prepared. The top photographs show procedures to follow on entering the area, and the lower ones show procedures on leaving.

to display something that they know to benefit both themselves and others.

A similar phenomenon can be identified for compliance with rules. Whereas the traditional approach displayed rules especially when people did not obey them, groups now display the rules that they themselves create and uphold.

The presence of suitable documentation within employees' territory changes the manner in which they perceive it. Displaying messages does not represent an external constraint; instead, it symbolizes a commitment on the part of the group.

Additional Advantages

In addition to the psychological aspect, encouraging employees to participate in a visual documentation project provides two practical advantages.

One advantage, quality, arises from the fact that visual documentation is a product like any other product. The employees are consumers. Obtaining their participation in designing the product is the most effective way to ensure high-quality results. An effective approach consists of forming a study group of representatives from various departments. After a trial period, meeting with employees and conducting surveys in work areas can provide feedback on forms of communication.

Second, the responsibilities of some departments are reduced. At the Hewlett-Packard plant in Fort Collins, Colorado, a group of four employees has specific responsibility for managing workplace documentation. One of them said, "The engineers oversaw the initial phase of this project, but now they trust us and they don't stick their noses into what we're doing any more."

Moderated Participation

While acknowledging the need to involve employees systematically in displaying information and instructions, one must find methods suitable for each situation. Because visual documentation covers an extremely broad range — from manufacturing tolerances defined by the design department to colored markings on machines for lubrication points — participation by production teams must be moderated. There are two general types of documents.

Certain documents can be completed entirely by the production units, including most simple documents that do not require centralized storage of information. Other documents should remain under the control of administrative departments. Nevertheless, even in this instance the administration should try to maintain a cooperative relationship with the users. Accept from the start that the design of a document with original information will be supplemented by employees as they use the document.

To ensure completion of these instructions, provide a space on each sheet for supplementary information. Another method with display boards provides open areas next to standard documents so that teams can record additional information they consider useful.

4

Visual Production Control

During the 1970s and 1980s, when the West was seeking to fathom the enigma of Japanese competitiveness, entrepreneurs returning from a visit to Toyota reported that they had encountered an odd production control method. This rather archaic-seeming process, known as kanban, used cards that traveled between work stations (kanban means "card" in Japanese).

The western visitors smiled condescendingly. "These fellows are tough to beat on prices, because they pay low salaries and they never take vacations. Fortunately, when it comes to managing production, they can't hold a candle to us. We can computerize our factories. Their state of the art is the abacus."

Nearly ten years later, when I visited the NUMMI factory in California, William Borton, at that time manager of the stamping plant, began his presentation by saying, "Our production control methods rely heavily on visual control. In the stamping unit, we are managing production and inventory without a computer."

There was a certain pride in his voice. Nevertheless, as a resident of Silicon Valley, Borton did not disdain computers. He merely meant that his plant had adopted a particular mode of organization in which the cry to computerize everything had been abandoned. Computers were being used only in carefully selected situations.

To understand NUMMI's outlook — which many other firms have adopted — we must recognize that during the 1970s and 1980s, computer technology appeared to be a miracle cure for managing the complex problems of production units. Today, an impasse has arisen, derived from two fundamental errors.

The first error was not to question the reasons for the level of complexity. Companies blindly relied on the power of their computer hardware, when they might better have invested more energy in simplifying modes of organization.

The second error consisted of attempting to achieve optimum plant control while not developing the relationship between production personnel and logistics systems. The quality of communication between the people engaged in production and the information systems guiding them became unimportant.

Visual production control differs fundamentally from this perspective. Simultaneously, visual production control contributes to simplification of decision-making systems and to broader employee participation in managing production units.

WHAT IS VISUAL PRODUCTION CONTROL?

Production control consists of orienting production units according to well-defined directions. Quantities and deadline objectives must be defined, and decisions must be made for ordering raw materials and parts, allocating human and technical resources, starting the manufacturing process at the proper time, and selecting priorities in the event of overloading of production units.

How does adding the adjective "visual" change the way of maintaining control? Consider examples from everyday life.

A motorist uses visual control when she drives her automobile according to what she sees: breakdown indicators, signal lights, the line of cars in front of her, turning lanes, and road markings. A pedestrian uses visual control when he wends his way through a city, walking on the sidewalks or protected walkways, and waiting for a signal light to cross an intersection.

A consumer uses visual control in preparing a shopping list according to the amounts of provisions in the pantry. A cook in a fast food restaurant uses visual control to prepare hamburgers after noticing that the small reserve supply near the counter is dwindling.

Are these situations "visual production control"? Is it acting solely on the basis of what one sees? The answer to this question is not so simple. Although in certain instances, visual production control can be defined in this way (and therefore precludes assistance from a computer), these situations do not constitute a general rule.

Although it is easy to imagine a baker visually checking his supply of chocolate blocks, this procedure would be insufficient in a factory where 20,000 components must be handled in an automatic storage warehouse. Even in computerized warehouses, however, it is possible to practice visual inventory control.

Visual production control does not necessarily mean returning to the Stone Age. When an airplane pilot decides to switch to visual control, she does not disconnect every computer on board. Two more examples will help develop another definition.

A CARD GAME

Today, the kanban method has become familiar in the West to manage production processes that occur in repetitive series. The basic principle of kanban is explained by Figure 4-1.

Kanban is a good example of visual production control because it relies on a system of cards arranged on a board. As the level of cards with a particular reference number begins to rise, the need to resume production is immediately clear.

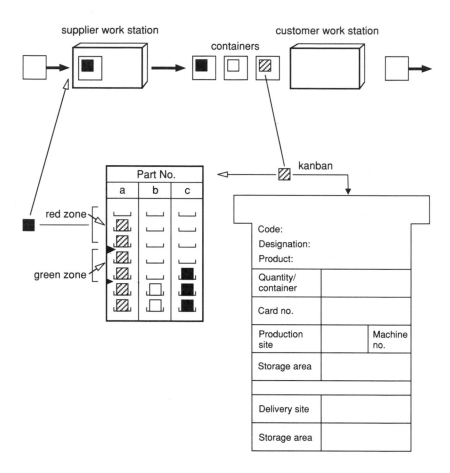

Figure 4-1. A kanban system. Each subsequent work station (customer) maintains a small permanent supply of containers for various components delivered by the previous work station (supplier). A kanban card always accompanies each container delivered. When the customer depletes a container, the card is sent to the supplier, which treats the card as an order and produces the required components. Decisions to start production are the sole prerogative of the customer and the supplier; the central office is not involved. The late Taiichi Ohno, the inventor of the system, compared it to the self-service concept in supermarkets.

Assume that the board has been replaced by a computer screen. The data remains the same and the cards are merely processed by the computer system. Is visual control still occurring?

Going one step further, assume that the computer that is processing these "electronic kanbans" will henceforth receive sales projections from the marketing division and that these figures will be represented on the screen by directions to the operator about the priority for resuming production of one item or another. Using this computer support, clearly the system is highly sophisticated. It is not totally manual. Is visual control still taking place?

This difficulty in defining the precise limits of visual control demonstrates that we have veered onto an incorrect course. We have been seeking a definition oriented toward the means of visual control, when what we need is a definition derived from the relationship between the people and the system.

What makes kanban a visual control system is not the techniques employed to display data. The vital aspect is the form of the worker's accessibility to logistical information. Like visual communication, visual production control is control by visibility.

Such visibility depends on three fundamental rules:

- Situations are visible to everyone.
- Goals and rules are visible to everyone.
- Each person participates and considers himself or herself involved.

Situations are Visible to Everyone

Anyone can determine the number of unfilled orders — the amount of work needed by a client work station — by observing the height of the row of cards. The row closest to the warning threshold indicates an item needed on a priority basis. Delays are immediately visible, because if the cards are in the red area

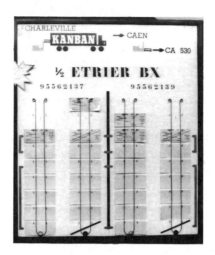

Figure 4-2. Kanban board at the Citroën plant in Caen. This board holds kanban tickets used to order parts delivered by another plant. Tickets are not physically returned to the supplier; to reduce delays, they are sent by telecopier. The operator who will use the particular items does the telecopying.

and the item is not yet being produced, everyone understands that the situation is critical.

William Borton of the NUMMI plant provides this anecdote:

> One day a fork lift driver came to see me, very upset. He said that as he passed by the semifinished stamped parts, he noticed that there were only enough parts for half an hour of production. Then a shutdown would be necessary. A quick investigation showed that the kanban ticket had been misplaced. Keeping track of inventory wasn't one of the driver's usual functions. Because the parts were systematically arranged and because he knew the warning level, however, he could easily detect the problem. Without his action, a welding shop shutdown would certainly have been necessary, with drastic technical and financial consequences.

Goals and Rules Are Visible to Everyone

The first objective is to avoid causing the client — the downstream work station — to halt production. This goal becomes a criterion for the upstream work station's turnaround time, which is the maximum period of time allowable for delivering an order when interruption of production is imminent. The turnaround time is visible on the kanban board: It is the distance separating the red indicator from the maximum height of the row of cards.

The second objective is to limit quantities of semifinished items. The maximum level that must not be exceeded is visible as the total height of the row, which indicates the number of tickets in circulation.

The operating rules for the system are also visible. To ensure that everyone can see them, some companies print their rules in large letters on the board where the cards are placed: "No kanbans, no production." "No containers without kanbans." "Put the proper number of items in each container."

Each Person Participates

The word "participation" means that everyone can see exactly how the kanban system operates. Everyone understands its objectives, requirements, and rules. Everyone becomes capable of participating in daily decisions (starting production according to the number of cards) and in discussions related to the criteria for these decisions.

For example, if the required time for exchanging a tool on a machine has just been reduced, removing some of the cards is unquestionably one of the unit supervisor's options (to reduce the inventory of semifinished items). Nevertheless, the supervisor does not make this decision without the participation of the person normally assigned to the work station.

In contrast, if a machine is unreliable, the unit supervisor might add several cards to gain a safety margin. In each instance, the employees who are involved take part in weighing the decisions.

A RETURN TO WALL SCHEDULES

Kanban is a highly decentralized and unusually simple control method, but its applicability is limited to essentially continuous logistical processes — standard products with a smooth demand. To understand visual control in situations that require more complex scheduling, consider the situation of a job shop unit that manufactures small quantities of various items.

At its plant in Cholet, France, Ernault Toyota produces digitally controlled machinery and machining systems. The production process for a given machine is relatively complex, but has two principal phases: machining components and assembling them. We will examine the production unit where parts are machined. Note that in a small-lot production unit, the same machines cannot be permanently assigned to the same items. Each machine must work on many different items in succession.

The scheduling problem is similar to the problem of driving through a city in an automobile — there are numerous intersections. In a factory, it is difficult to create a detailed schedule of the flow of parts, and production lead times frequently become a problem. The situation differs significantly from the simple rules that govern application of a method such as kanban.

According to the plant's operations manager, the machining unit found it difficult to meet specified deadlines. To know how much time was needed for starting production was nearly impossible. A tendency developed, therefore, to plan more output than was needed. This approach offered a safety buffer, but it also created delays; as work-in-process accumulated, completion times became entirely unpredictable.

"Our production orders noted dates," the operations manager told me, "but the dates were regarded more as wishes than commitments. I remember the day I asked the unit supervisor why a particular production run had been delayed for two weeks. Completely calm, he replied, 'Why, that's normal. Nobody ever complained about it before.'"

Visual Aids

Missed deadlines may be quite familiar to some readers. The Ernault Toyota operations manager describes how the plant surmounted the problem:

> The system was based on faulty logic. We changed it entirely. Instead of viewing deadlines as consequences of the production unit's operations, we defined them as rules to be obeyed.
>
> We gave the machining unit a certain amount of latitude in organizing scheduling for its machines, managing priorities, and allocating its resources. In exchange for more autonomy, the machining unit committed itself to a time frame of ten days between its initial and final procedures.[1]
>
> As soon as precise responsibilities were contractually established, the unit found it necessary to indicate the status of production in an explicit form. That is why wall schedules reappeared in the work area. (see Figure 4-3)

---

[1] Instead of committing itself to a final deadline, the unit selected a time frame between initial and final procedures. The distinction is fundamental, because a production unit cannot promise the same deadline regardless of the quantity of incoming orders. If the work load assigned to a unit matches its capabilities, the team can firmly commit itself to a flow period and honor its commitment. Thus, the scheduling unit becomes responsible for ensuring that workloads do not exceed production capability. Orders placed to the left of the date in the left portion of the chart indicate possible excess workloads. (See Figure 4-3)

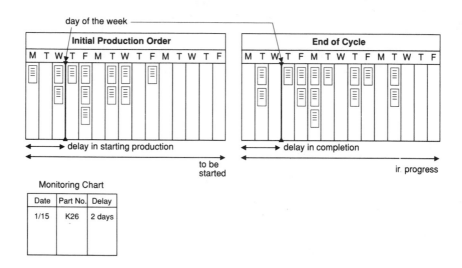

Figure 4-3. Schedule for machining orders, Ernault Toyota factory, Cholet, France. The chart has two sections, each a calendar representing the same two-week period.

Production orders (tickets issued by the assembly unit) are placed on the left side of the chart, in the row for the specified day for the first operation for each order. When that operation has occurred, the ticket is moved to the right side, within exactly ten days (the stipulated period). It is especially easy to interpret this chart:

• Tickets on the left side of the chart indicate the orders that have not been started: the workload for subsequent days. Tickets on the left of the current date (marked by a red line) indicate a delay in starting production.

• Tickets on the right side of the chart indicate orders in progress. Orders appearing to the left of the line for the date should already have been finished. These orders are overdue.

The monitoring chart is used to identify orders in progress likely to be delayed. Detecting delays involves monitoring of completion dates for certain benchmark procedures.

Communication with our production units has completely changed. We are no longer content to have plans drawn up by an office that sees itself as the brain of the company. Situations are discussed in work areas with the people who actually work in production. Standing in front of the charts, we all have access to the same information.

The results have met our highest expectations. After several months, the time frame was reduced to ten days, whereas the average had previously gone as high as thirty days. (Figure 4-3)

The advantages of this new distribution of responsibilities are clear. Time frames are honored; the central scheduling unit no longer needs to monitor in detail the progress of operations. It trusts the team in the machining unit. The scheduling unit is merely informed of potential delays and overloads. It can control by exception — that is, only in situations that deviate strongly from the standard.

Three Rules for Visual Control

Ernault Toyota's machining shop is especially relevant because, unlike kanban, it does not involve a wholly visual decision-making system. The ongoing status of production stages is not detailed on the chart for each machine. The computer retains its role as a scheduling aid. Only the ultimate results are observable. Nevertheless, this system constitutes visual production control, upholding the three rules developed in the discussion of kanban:

1. At any time a glance at a chart will give anyone an idea of the actual situation in relation to the standard. Consulting the chart for delayed orders is sufficient. A glance also suffices for determining the current workload, namely, orders that must be started, as well as the portion of production that is backed up.

2. The rules of visual production control are visible. In this instance, the rule is to respect the established ten-day time frame between the initial and final steps in producing a given lot, and to prevent work-in-process from accumulating in excess of a specified level.

3. The machining team participates in logistical control. In the first place, it is involved in daily operations, because upholding the time frame is one of its goals, on a par with quality or productivity. Moreover, the team is involved in evaluating the effectiveness of the control system. The time frame is not an obligation that a central scheduling unit imposes in a disjointed way. The ten-day time frame is derived from consensus.

Summary

The variety of situations in the realm of operations makes it risky to define visual production control generally. The two examples identified a variable and a constant:

- The variable is the extent to which the display of information plays a role in the decision-making process. When inventories are regulated with a double-compartment method, visual inventory control is occurring. When a computer-generated production schedule is displayed, visual control also occurs. (Figure 4-7)
- The constant is the nature of the relationship between employees and the operations system. The three fundamental rules for visual production control summarize this relationship. (Figure 4-4)

Visual production control is less a matter of algorithms than of communication. If Ernault Toyota's wall schedule remains in the supervisor's office, visual control no longer exists. If a warehouse employee receives instructions to order mer-

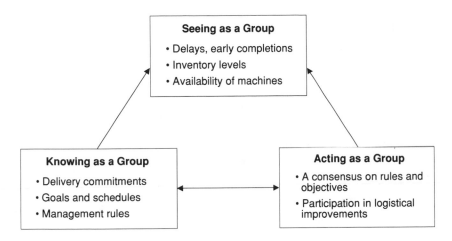

Figure 4-4. The visual control triangle.

chandise according to visible inventory levels on the shelves, but we forget to ask her to mark the shelves with the resupply thresholds that appear on the list she zealously keeps in her pocket, visual production control is no longer taking place.

When factories eliminated wall schedules and turned to computers, they committed a grave error. Charts are decision-making tools. We forgot that they are also communication tools and symbols.

Most companies considered only the technical aspects of logistical problems in the past. The communications dimension was completely obscured.[2] Visual production control innovatively introduces a role for communication between human beings and the logistical system in industrial planning.

---

[2] A computer is a valuable tool for individual communication, but not for group communication — it lacks public interface. When computers can offer expanded visibility (displaying data on illuminated boards, graphic displays for inventories and flows), they will play a larger role in visual control for production units.

Today, many firms are attempting to pursue the visual communication path. They are discovering advantages: simplification of production-control systems, more effective distribution of responsibilities, greater coherence in decision making, and effectiveness in terms of scheduling. The remaining portion of this chapter will describe practical procedures that permit application of this approach. These procedures are organized in six stages:

- Building a consensus
- Defining priority objectives
- Decentralizing the decision-making system
- Creating visual schedules
- Choosing simple methods
- Displaying the results

BUILDING A CONSENSUS

The principal activity of France Abonnements is to provide newspaper subscriptions to the general public at reduced rates. The processing center in Chantilly, France, processes administrative records. Its deadline problems, however, are completely similar to those of a manufacturing company. As in a factory, random factors may affect the flow of administrative records: the unforeseen arrival of a wave of new files, personnel shortages, bottlenecks, incomplete subscriber files, and so on.

Like every growing company, France Abonnements experienced problems with delays during particular periods. Sometimes more than two weeks elapsed between the arrival and updating of a particular file, whereas other files could be processed in a few days, without anyone knowing why. Michele Pilhan, the department manager, decided that the delays could be resolved only if a limit was established:

It's useless to say "We'll improve our time." A precise goal must be set, and the means of achieving it must be provided. After consultations with department managers (during several months), a two-day deadline was established. During the preparation phase, informal contacts with the entire staff took place.

That point required the most attention. Our reasoning was based on customers who had to be satisfied. In our business, one satisfied subscriber often means two new subscribers. By talking about these topics, everyone gradually came to understand that processing time was a strategic goal for the future of our company.

Arrangements were made to ensure that the two-day deadline could actually be met. Above all, it was essential not to risk failure. When everything had been completely prepared, we held a general meeting. The two-day deadline was officially declared the target deadline. This goal seemed ambitious, and some people had doubts about the success of the program. Everyone was prepared to pursue it, however, and to accept the idea of changing old work habits.

To depict this decision, and to provide a concrete image of the commitment, we had two stickers made. These are attached to every container of subscribers' files. One indicates the target date in large numbers. Therefore, everyone can see whether or not a given deadline will be met. The other sticker shows a symbol of the collective commitment. (Figure 4-5)

This method essentially relieves me of one concern — monitoring deadlines. Most of the necessary steps are performed by the staff itself. Not only is the two-day deadline regularly fulfilled, but it has become so habitual that no one would say, "There's a problem, but, too bad, there's going to be a little delay." That would be as inappropriate as intentionally sending correspondence to an incorrect address.

The example of France Abonnements demonstrates that applying a visual communication system for managing records — displaying the two-day goal on the trays and visually monitoring the flow of records — resulted from carefully executed preparations. The firm's management did not merely order stickers and decorate each tray. Before launching the program, it

Figure 4-5. File trays at the Chantilly facility of France Abonnements.
Stickers attached to the trays tell the date that materials are put in the tray
and reaffirm the companywide commitment to respond within two days.

convinced the employees that the deadline was crucially important to the company.

Displaying information played a role only because a consensus was created before the program started. Posting stickers
indicating "two days to respond" without prior agreement would
have been useless.

DEFINING PRIORITY OBJECTIVES

When a marketing manager sends a schedule to a production manager, he indicates the quantities of each item to produce by certain dates. Communication is not limited to the
numbers, however. An implicit understanding exists between
the two about the meaning of the numbers, as a result of their
working relationship.

Without needing to specify, these managers know how to distinguish between the indispensable and the merely desirable, and between items that may cause difficulties in export markets in the event of delays and items that will remain in the firm's inventories for an extended period. If priorities must be changed, nothing prevents them from communicating by telephone to modify schedules. Their mutual knowledge of the context complements the initial information and allows them to interpret it properly.

The situation is different when schedules are posted in work areas. Raw figures are visible. When a schedule is placed on a wall, each individual understands it in his or her own way. The author is absent and cannot govern the process of interpretation.

Interpretations, however, may be wholly at odds. When the text reads "Goal: to produce 400 items in one day," what does it mean?

- Is it a pious wish intended to stimulate more intense efforts, even though everyone knows that the schedule is always overly ambitious?
- Is it a minimum figure that should normally be surpassed, with a bonus as encouragement?
- Is it a goal that may be waived if necessary, as a result of financial considerations (not shutting down the machining section, giving priority to manufacturing products with higher value, and so on)?

Three Golden Rules of Displayed Objectives

If ambiguities about the meaning of displayed information persist it is impossible to mobilize a group. Everyone who notices a figure on a chart must perceive it in the same way and believe that the same perception exists for the entire group. Three conditions are required for this degree of uniform perception:

1. The objective must be realistic. It must be attainable in terms of the available resources and the organization's rules.

How can a group be motivated with productivity levels that in most situations are unattainable? Nothing is accomplished by displaying a quantity that is challenged every other day because an upstream unit is not delivering suitable components, or because inspection procedures are halting questionable deliveries.

If a production unit is incapable of meeting a given goal, it is better not to display any goal. At least, the symbolic properties of visual space (the sense of being confronted by reality, described in Chapter 1) can be preserved for the future.[3]

2. The objective must be precisely defined, with a predetermined level of accuracy.

In traditional management, a production goal is always understood as "the more you can do, the better you are." In a visual organization this is not a good message, because it cannot be understood in the same way by everyone.

Visual communication needs to be unequivocal in its context; otherwise it is not a common language. If a goal is posted, it must be reached — no less, no more.[4]

---

[3] This requirement — displaying only reasonable objectives — will be discussed in relation to performance indicators in Chapter 6.

[4] Possible improvements should be preceded by modification of goals. Japanese production specialists strongly emphasize the need to stabilize the operating system in relation to a reasonable objective before introducing more ambitious objectives. Before moving a target further away, it is first necessary to learn how to hit the bull's-eye.

3. Finally, objectives that are to be displayed must be included among the priority objectives that guide the
organization as a whole. The financial considerations
on every executive's mind (cost reductions for materials,
effective personnel use, optimum value added) should
not interfere with approved programs.

Clearly, these justifiable considerations exist for every
company. Financial considerations should be taken into account
before displaying target quantities, not afterwards.

For displayed information to be effective, all the elements
of a problem must be visible. In other words, whatever is displayed must always be more important than undisplayed information.

A Cultural Transformation

These three rules show the similarity between a displayed
production quantity and a quality standard. Like a quality
specification (dimensions and tolerances for machined parts,
for example), the figures on a chart must simultaneously be realistic, accurate, and top priority.

Most companies do not accept the idea that deadlines,
schedules, and inventories of work-in-process are standards.
Instead, people tend to say: "You'll have it as soon as possible,"
or "Production time? That depends, it's hard to say," or "Work-
in-process? It's impossible to plan. There are so many factors
involved." Not only are attempts to achieve a standard for
quantities produced by individual production units lacking, but
there is an effort to do exactly the opposite. Throughout the
plant, people regularly evade the standards for improving output at individual work stations.

Companies that display logistical information have adopted
an entirely different approach, as with France Abonnements.
Imagine if a new employee who asked about the meaning of the

stickers posted on trays were told: "Oh, those things! The former marketing manager put them there so that the files would move faster, but that never worked very well. Since she left, they're just used for decoration."

Visual control at France Abonnements is successful only because the employees speak in an entirely different way. A new employee is told: "You see what is indicated on every tray. The house rule is that files must be available in two days." In only a few days a new employee understands that the file-processing system was designed for this purpose and that the entire staff tries to meet this goal, which is truly a companywide standard.

New employees recognize immediately that they are working for a firm where messages are not displayed merely for appearances. If stickers remain on all of the trays, it is because the conditions have been brought together to make the goal of "Two days to respond" both feasible and obligatory.

A fundamental principle therefore underlies the term "standard": goals should be displayed only when it is possible for the goal to take on the status of a collective reference point. A clear reference point must be devoid of ambiguity and arbitrariness, and accepted by everyone. Failure to observe these requirements — posting messages without providing a decoding key — is like mounting a clock for a different time zone in a work area.

DECENTRALIZING THE DECISION-MAKING PROCESS

The manner in which a wall schedule was used for planning in the machining unit of Ernault Toyota in Cholet, France, was described earlier. The next example describes inventory-control methods for certain components awaiting assembly. (Figure 4-6)

Until the past few years, components were stored in a central warehouse. Today, most of them are stored near the assembly lines. The instructions for the machining unit for a given

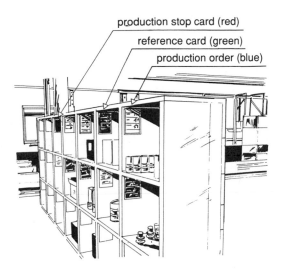

Figure 4-6. Decentralized inventory control in the assembly area of the Ernault Toyota plant, Cholet, France.

manufacturing process are placed on the side of each bin; these instructions are on a blue ticket. A green ticket is placed behind the blue ticket as a precaution. The green ticket contains designations for different items as well as the parameters that define the inventory-control rules: the threshold that supplies must reach before an order will be issued, the amount to be ordered, and the time frame. When an assembler draws from the reserve inventory (at the bottom of the rack, separate from other components), the blue ticket must be sent to the machining unit. This ticket is attached to the chart in Figure 4-3. If supplies have reached a zero level, the assembler must turn the green card over; the other side is red.

This inventory-control system meets the three basic requirements for visual control:

- The rule for initiating an order is visible: It is written on the green ticket, which remains on the rack. Anyone who passes by is informed and can determine whether the rule is being applied.

- A high level of employee involvement exists. Assembly personnel are responsible for monitoring their inventory, issuing tickets, and alerting the operations manager in certain predetermined situations. If the inventory control rules must be changed (for example, to raise the minimum inventory level), assembly personnel participate in the decision.
- A more visual system is difficult to imagine. By passing by the racks, anyone can immediately determine the general condition of inventories. Many blue tickets indicate that the inventory level is rising. If there are more green tickets than usual, the inventory level is dwindling. "Seeing red" is a warning: The inventory level has entered a critical phase and the machining unit is no longer meeting the assembly unit's needs.

The Supervisor's Viewpoint

Consider the opinion of the head of the assembly team in regard to functioning of the new inventory control system:

Previously, the computer issued a list for the warehouse. At certain times, I'd receive large quantities of components, and the workers would ask, "Where can we put all this stuff?" Then the pallets had to be moved, and some inventory had to be stored in the aisles.

On other occasions, because the warehouse was swamped with several orders on the same day, I didn't receive what I had requested. I had to go in person to the warehouse and wait to be served. Then, because the parts were all mixed together and loose in the same crate, I sometimes discovered errors in the order and had to return to the warehouse to look for the missing parts.

Now the procedure has been changed. Every work station must be responsible for its own inventory. I remember that the workers were rather hesitant at first. They said: "You want us to keep an eye on the warehouse so that we'll be held responsible," but after a few months of operating this way, they saw that things were running more smoothly. This is a practical, visible system that functions independently, and one clear advantage is that the workers assume responsibility for their own supplies.

Before, between the time spent running after parts and filling out papers, I wasn't able to attend to immediate problems and to organize our work. Now, I'm not being interrupted all the time. I can devote much more time to technical matters and improvements.

A Question of Trust

When a company is considering the necessary preconditions for decentralizing inventory control for production units, one major objection is often raised. "The workers will take too much at a time. They'll make mistakes with the coding. Bad parts will be mixed in with good parts. It's going to be complete chaos. Why should they manage inventory?"

Many companies are reluctant to decentralize operating functions. They prefer to maintain cumbersome administrative procedures instead of allowing production units to manage portions of their own inventory control. When managers are asked about the reason for this reluctance, they often cite a lack of trust.

Like the Ernault Toyota factory, many other factories are proving such apprehensions unfounded. Visual communication plays a decisive role in a process that contributes to restoring trust. Two principal factors are involved.

The first factor is simplicity of communication. Use of concrete reference points, vivid symbols, colors, and so on reduces the risk of unintentional errors.

The second factor concerns errors that may be intentional or arise from negligence. If regulated systems and monitoring methods are well planned, signs that express rules and ways of following them will be extremely clear. People have fear of being caught flouting rules that are displayed in common areas. They fear being excluded from the group because violations — which can hardly be considered unwitting, with the exceptional clarity of the signs — challenge the basic rules governing the visual territory.

With this form of public organization, as with mechanisms to maintain traffic control in cities or on roads, autonomy depends on absolute compliance with visible rules. As in urban space, visual organization within a plant establishes a favorable context for collective self-control, thereby creating conditions for functioning in a more decentralized manner.[5]

CREATING VISUAL SCHEDULES

When a company operates on the basis of quantities scheduled for production in a given period instead of on batch orders, it must display the amounts required and the amounts actually produced, rather than indicating the date when a production run must be completed.

The following recommendations relate to the design of display media:

- Charts indicating required and completed quantities should be situated in the team's space. These charts should be visible not only to workers within the unit, but to anyone passing through.

---

[5] The visible indicators that express the rules of urban space are effective even in the absence of witnesses. Why do people obey traffic lights at night, even when there are no cars on intersecting streets? Because these indicators constitute an attribute of urban space. Running a red light is not merely disobeying an abstract law, but denying that a city is public space.

- Messages should be as clear as possible. Colors should be used effectively. For example, goals can be expressed in blue and levels of implementation in red. Figures should stand out.
- To simplify the process, a prearranged layout is advisable, with predetermined columns, titles, and boxes. When certain entries or symbols reappear regularly, place them on magnetic cards that can be rearranged.
- Pay considerable attention to the appearance, format, and colors of different portions of the chart. Remember that a schedule symbolizes a team's contribution to the company's strategic objective: serving its clients better.
- Choose acknowledgment indicators or symbols, to emphasize the fulfillment of objectives more effectively. In some firms, a sun, a star, or a colored sticker is posted when a standard is attained, for positive reinforcement.
- Employees should participate in designing the charts. A small study group can assume responsibility for this activity, with he appropriate departments.
- Finally, a team should enter its own figures on charts. "The workers wouldn't give up their right to enter their results on the chart for anything in the world," a manager at Ernault Toyota said. "The moment when a worker places a yellow sticker on the chart to confirm that the schedule has been met has now become part of the daily routine. A figure that a team member enters awkwardly is much more relevant for the intended purpose than an overly sophisticated document produced by a printer."

CHOOSING SIMPLE METHODS

The examples in this chapter are so simple that one wonders why companies did not apply these methods earlier. But simplicity is not easy to attain, either from an organizational standpoint (since it usually requires decentralizing) or from the

daily schedule

daily production

Figure 4-7. Weekly schedule at the Télémécanique factory in Carros.
The production teams are responsible for monitoring the weekly schedule.
Brief daily meetings allow a review of the schedule and develop consensus
for necessary measures.

standpoint of the company culture. Imagine the reaction of a
Western executive in the 1970s on hearing a proposal to manage
a plant using the kanban method.

Solex provides an example of simple visual control procedures. Formerly, all carburetor components were stored in a
warehouse. To meet production units' needs, Solex established
lots at the point when production began. Massive deliveries of
components to each production unit therefore cluttered the areas
around the assembly locations. Furthermore, if the schedule
changed, the unused items had to be returned to the warehouse.

Today, assembly stations store components in small units
on rollers that contain numerous compartments, with two iden-
tical compartments for each component. When a compartment
is empty, it is sent to the warehouse to be filled. This procedure
simplifies supplying of assembly areas. Shutdowns and over-
supply problems no longer occur because components are de-

Figure 4-8. Citroën plant in Caen. When oil is needed, the order is placed when the operator moves the disk suspended from a small chain to the placard indicating oil requirements. Then the warehouse worker completes a delivery during usual rounds.

The lower left portion of the chart indicates the meaning of symbols used on the machines (draining, manual lubrication, pressure gauge, and so on). The cards confirm deliveries for administrative purposes. The safety poster at the lower right warns against lubrication while the machine is running.

livered only as they are needed. The procedure is simple, and even new workers can follow it without error.

This approach has resulted in extensively upgraded inventory control because warehouse personnel have gained more time for supplying special components precisely and promptly.

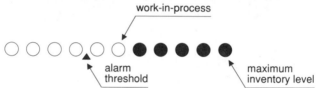

Figure 4-9. Hewlett-Packard Plant in Cupertino, California. This chart regulates the flow between the unit that manufactures circuit boards and the unit that assembles subsystems. There are several horizontal rows of magnetic disks, with one for every subassembly part number. Each disk represents a group of boards needed to prepare a subassembly. The disk has two sides, red and green. When a series is started, the red side of each disk is visible. The production unit manufactures the first boards in accordance with the computerized schedule.

When a group of boards is ready, the unit that produces boards turns the disk so that the green side faces upward. The production unit that assembles subsystems checks the chart regularly to determine availability of materials, according to the green disks. When a batch of circuit boards is taken to subassembly, the disk is turned back to the red side. At the same time, a standardized order is sent to the warehouse to initiate the preparation of component kits for assembling the boards. All flows are recorded by a computer.

This system is similar to kanban but is better suited to small-lot production under a schedule.

Figure 4-10. The kanban squares method, Hewlett-Packard, Cupertino.
This method is nicknamed "kanban squares" because the spaces marked on
the floor occupy the same role as kanban cards in authorizing upstream
production. All of the systems being assembled must be placed in squares
marked on the floor. When a team observes that a square is open, it prepares
the subassemblies for the next computer. This simple concept embodies a
common-sense approach, like waiting for an opening before pulling one's car
out into traffic.

DISPLAYING RESULTS

Ernault Toyota's system for visually displaying production
starts for machined parts includes a graph that records performance levels for the unit on a regular basis. (Figure 4-13)

This document is important for several réasons. First, its
existence proves that the deadline has become a standard. The
company measures deviations from the schedule in exactly the
same way it measures deviations from product quality standards. Second, the graph permits evaluation of the efficiency of
the operating system. Everyone can see how the production unit
is meeting its commitments. The employees discuss it regularly.

stamping presses

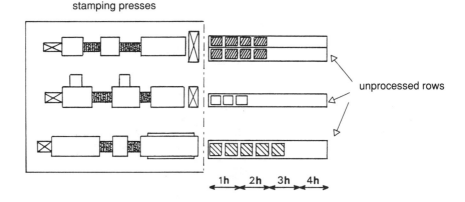

Figure 4-11. The stamping unit at the NUMMI plant, Fremont, California.
This communication system is based on positions of objects on the floor.
Loads of steel for the stamping unit are placed at the entrance to the area
where the presses are located. The widths of the areas set aside for each
category of steel are selected to correspond to a four-hour supply of steel.
The area occupied by unprocessed sheets is thus proportional to the inventory flow rate. Since the flow can be monitored, by observing the sheets of
steel, anyone can monitor inventory levels.

Simply gathering in front of the chart encourages them to suggest improvements.

Finally, the graph is included within an agreement of trust.
As soon as a planning device has been deemed effective, the op-
erations department no longer needs to monitor events closely.
The graph will show performance levels.

(a) With a colored scale behind the reels, inventory levels can be determined visually. If the red zone never appears, there is excess inventory.

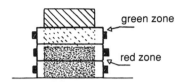

green zone

red zone

(b) Lots arriving at the warehouse are arranged in transit areas according to arrival dates. Delays in receiving goods can therefore be detected immediately.

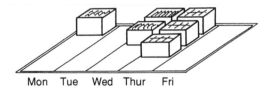

Mon   Tue   Wed   Thur   Fri

(c) Each week a disk with a different color is placed on the identification cards for containers when production begins. Thus, delayed production runs are immediately identifiable.

Production starts, week 23   Production starts, week 24   Production starts, week 25

(d) The width of the area allocated for each category is proportional to the quantity sold. Thus the height represents the flow period for remaining inventory. Parts that are approaching the alert threshold can be seen at a glance.

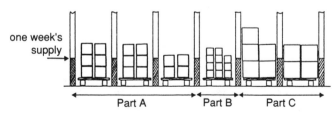

one week's supply

Part A   Part B   Part C

Note: These examples are provided as illustrations. In practice, application requires research in advance, because it depends on the specific logistical problems of the situation.

Figure 4-12. Several ways to represent production flows

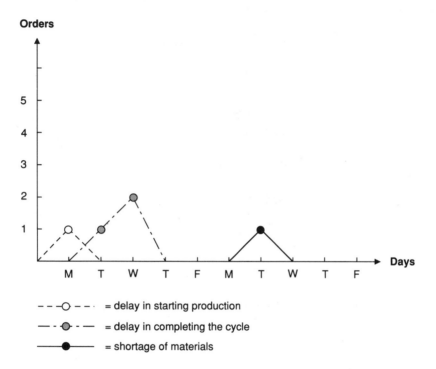

Orders

Figure 4-13. Delay graph for the machining unit at the Ernault Toyota plant. Three sources of delay are monitored. They form the basis for three curves in different colors: delays in starting, delays in completing an order, and delays attributable to shortages of materials.

Figure 4-14. Inventory graph in the component storage area at the Télé-mécanique plant in Carros. The curve of unavailable items measures the effectiveness of the service provided. The warehouse worker merely enters the numbers of items that could not be supplied at the required time during a given month. This curve is displayed in the warehouse. When the supervisors must discuss the problem of unavailable items, they can meet where the problem is encountered most immediately, with the principal interested parties. If decisions must be made, all parties can commit themselves.

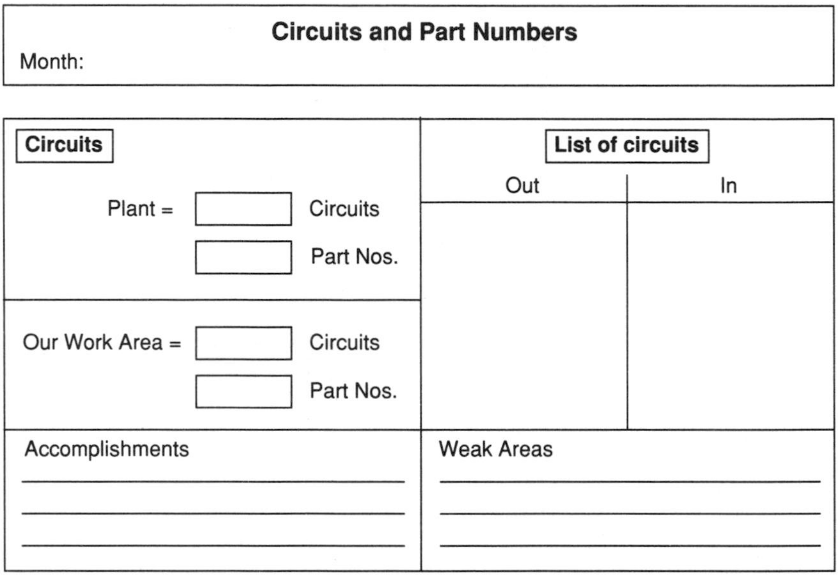

Circuits and Part Numbers

Month:

Circuits

Plant = [ ] Circuits

[ ] Part Nos.

Our Work Area = [ ] Circuits

[ ] Part Nos.

Accomplishments

_____
_____
_____

List of circuits

Out	In

Weak Areas

_____
_____
_____

Figure 4-15. Chart for implementing a kanban system, J. Reydel plant, Gondecourt. Introducing a kanban system is not enough. It is still necessary to ensure control of the system. This chart on the wall of the production unit is intended for that purpose. Control parameters (numbers of kanban routes, numbers of categories covered by kanbans, initial and final locations for parts) are entered on a regular basis. Weak points or problems to be solved are also recorded. Favorable results are recorded to provide encouragement. Everyone can observe how the kanban project is progressing throughout the plant.

5

Visual Quality Control

The manager of a plant that manufactures home appliances was dismayed by the number of items strewn on the floor in the work area. These small plastic parts had fallen off work tables or dollies. Although still usable, these parts were ultimately destined for the trash bin.

The manager was aware of the loss of money represented by these items. She attempted every means to persuade employees to change their ways — explanations to the employees' committee, memoranda to department heads, and posters placed around the work area. Hoping to set a good example for the employees, she even knelt on the floor to pick up fallen parts, but her efforts were in vain. Her words seemed to float over their heads.

Driving home one evening, an idea came to her — an original and audacious idea, but she thought it might work.

The next morning, the manager went to the bank and asked for 800 quarters. When she arrived at the plant, she strode into the work area and, like a farmer sowing a field, tossed the coins onto the floor.

The employees were shocked, and they stopped their work. The middle managers were baffled and wondered whether the boss had lost her mind. The plant manager placidly walked to her office. Twenty minutes later, her secretary indicated that the work area was in turmoil. A group consisting of the production manager, a supervisor, and two employee representatives was asking for a meeting.

She agreed to meet them immediately. When everyone was seated in her office, she said: "I've just reviewed the books. These 800 quarters represent the daily cost for parts that end up on the floor. Why didn't you come to me before, when the floor was covered with parts, instead of coins? The cost is exactly the same."

A SHARED PERCEPTION OF REALITY

This anecdote demonstrates that our perceptions of phenomena — and our reactions to them — depend upon our interpretations. When the manager walked through the work area strewn with parts, she saw shiny quarters about to be thrown into the trash. For the employees who worked in this area, parts lying on the floor were unimportant. The workers ceased to pay attention to them, as if they no longer saw them.

Seeing anomalies is the hardest task, according to Japanese industrial engineer Shigeo Shingo. He offers an anecdote:

> The slogan "Eliminate Waste" is posted in many plants I have visited. Once, when I saw this sign, I asked the firm's president if all his employees were idiots.
>
> "Why do you say that?" he responded. I pointed to the slogan posted on the wall.
>
> "But isn't it good to get rid of waste?" he asked. I asked him whether the sign was on the wall because some workers would not get rid of waste even if they saw it.
>
> "It seems to me," I said, "that as long as someone knows that something constitutes waste, he will get rid of it. The big problem is not noticing that something really *is* wasteful." The slogan posted, I told him, ought to be *"Find* Waste!"[1]

---

[1] Shingo, *Sayings*, op. cit. at 19-20.

Shingo is correct. Everyone who has been obliged to solve waste problems in an operational context knows that the hardest task, when minor problems of quality or efficiency arise, is not necessarily solving them, but seeing them. If seeing them becomes difficult — the lesson of the anecdote of the quarters — it is because we cease to regard them as problems. We become accustomed to them.

When we no longer worry about the things that we observe, when most anomalies are considered normal by the majority of workers in a company, from its chair to its employees, the firm is in jeopardy.

FACT-BASED COMMUNICATION

There are many ways to assign responsibility in a firm: according to products, functions, technology, or a matrix, and so on. Notwithstanding diverse expert opinions, only one way truly evinces unanimity. This approach consists of saying: "When things go well, it's because of me. When they don't go well, other people must be at fault."

How do we ask someone to observe reality — specifically the reality that emerges from unfavorable results — if the instinctive reaction is to consider oneself uninvolved? How will employees respond in the plant that Shingo visited if they feel blamed when they see panels reading "Find Waste"? Before introducing a visual control system, adopt careful measures for promoting calm discussion.

The goal is to introduce a more objective and less fault-finding mode of communication in the workplace. We must create a communication based on fact, not fault.

This observation does not imply that blame never exists, nor that individual responsibility should never be invoked. It is necessary, however, to distinguish carefully between moralistic and factual approaches. If the emotional content of the events that are to be observed has not been neutralized, a participant will not be able to observe his or her own actions.

The way in which charts are designed for recording quality problems on the assembly line at Sandouville clearly illustrates this quest for objectivity. (Figure 5-1) Although the results of a specific work station appear, the graph does not show the name of the person working at that location.

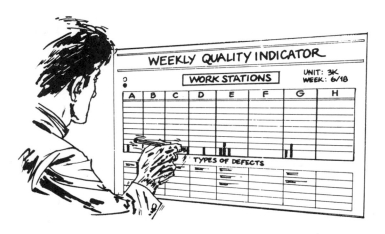

Figure 5-1. The Renault plant at Sandouville. The team's board summarizes defects observed during inspections of assembled work.

Is information displayed in this way anonymous? Does individual responsibility merge with collective responsibility? The process is more complex. When an assembly worker consults the chart, she is aware that the figures relate to her. This restrained approach, however, includes a fundamental principle: When deficiencies are communicated, workers recognize them as problems of the work station, not as deficiencies of a specific individual. In this way, everyone is capable of receiving information that may pertain to him or her.

There are many advantages to orienting messages toward work stations rather than to individuals. For instance, another assembly worker who may be assigned to the particular work station can open objective discussion more freely By contrast, if the name of an individual appeared on the chart, the other worker would form a negative opinion of his or her co-worker and might approach difficulties from a moral standpoint, although such an attitude is detrimental to seeking solutions for problems.

On the other hand, if the work station is the reference point, everyone can contribute by making suggestions about problems relevant to the entire group.

Thus, criticism can be more objective, more constructive, and less emotional.[2]

BURIED TREASURE

To advance from an environment dominated by blame to one based on trust and improvement cannot be accomplished in one day. Training may encourage a new way of speaking, but the attitude of top and middle management plays a critical role. Management must take responsibility for using emotions in a more effective way, taking the initiative to treat problems more objectively.

In particular, middle management is responsible for demonstrating that using problems as workplace opportunities will help initiate a progress-oriented process, a challenge to change. Showing that problems may be useful is the best way to

---

[2] To borrow an evocative expression from Edward de Bono's *Six Thinking Hats* (Boston: Little, Brown & Co., 1986), one must "put on a white hat" when developing systems for displaying information about quality. De Bono explains that effective communication requires agreement about the mode of communication participants adopt. To say that one is putting on a white hat is to announce one's intention of pursuing discussion based on facts. To say, "I'm putting on my red hat," indicates a desire to express feelings.

encourage the observational capabilities of employees at the immediate location.[3]

The Simpson Timber Company is one of the larger wood products firms in the United States. The solid wood division employs 3,000 people in an area near the coastal forests of Washington, Oregon, and California.

In recent years, the firm has undertaken a new strategy to improve all of the business basics — productivity, quality, and innovation. The strategy depends far more on mobilizing the employees to eliminate problems and defects, recognize opportunity, and increase the rate of systems innovation than on investments in technology.

Paul Everett is the project manager. Speaking to a group of operators and supervisors assembled for training in Value Adding Management, he said:

> Simpson employs people of many diverse talents — managers, administrators, engineers, maintenance experts and other technical personnel that have skills usually acquired through formal education. They have theoretical knowledge about wood, machinery, accounting, computers, and so on, as well as practical experience.
>
> What encourages me is that now we have, in value-adding management, the means to more fully utilize your practical knowledge gathered over the years while physically making our products. This great advantage — using all the talents of all of us — is the decisive action needed to secure our future at Simpson.

---

[3] Masaaki Imai states the same concept in *Kaizen* (New York: Random House, 1986), where he affirms that the first step is to prove to the entire organization that problems have a positive side. "There is a saying among [Total Quality Control] practitioners in Japan that problems are the keys to hidden treasure" (p. 163). The image of buried treasure is evocative. Everyone understands that a problem has two sides. One is negative: Production is disrupted. The other side is positive: The situation may offer information that may allow fuller understanding of the process and prevention of any recurrences of problems.

You are the only people who can directly observe what may be happening in a given situation. If a machine malfunctions, or a piece of lumber doesn't meet the specified tolerances, or there's a defect in some boards, who else is there when these events occur? Who else can perform real-time observation of these events? Who else can reach conclusions when events have just been observed in their natural environment and when they still reveal every element of their context?

This is what gives you a special role in the plant. You're the only people who encounter *real events*. If you want to learn a new way to see them, a new way to record them, and a new way to interpret them, we can convert them into progress together.

Production Is an Experimental Science

The view that workers on the front line are the foot-soldiers of progress conflicts with many traditional assumptions. Until recent years, whenever general managers were asked about efforts to advance manufacturing practices, they replied in terms of automated equipment, expansion of production capacity, larger storage facilities, remote controlled dollies, and so on.

Advances meant investing, and investing meant buying equipment, spending money to develop technologies or to purchase new machinery. It was difficult to envision progress without a large bill or several months of work by the technical division. Reducing proportions of defective items, curtailing excessive use of materials, and improving the positioning or reliability of machinery were never officially included within the scope of "progress." Companies appeared to show no interest in sources of productivity found in their own production units.

This tendency to downgrade progress in favor of improving current resources was based on an erroneous concept of production. Believing that optimum productivity could only be achieved from drawing-board models, managers rejected lessons found in attentive observation of processes. Events transpired as if production had become a theoretical science, whereas factory workers know that, to a significant degree, production is a science based on observation.

Until recently, companies that directed their efforts toward centralization and abstractions had simply ignored the experimental dimension of production.

Today, this new dimension of progress is being recognized.[4] Once understanding occurs, everything else follows naturally. Paul Everett is correct: Observing phenomena, paying attention to details, recording problems, searching for causes, and validating hypotheses are essential requirements for a firm seeking to improve constantly.

Summary

For an individual to observe his or her surroundings appears to be simple. Nevertheless, it is far more difficult for a group to arrive at a shared vision of reality.

The example of the plant whose floor was covered with parts showed that responses to problems depend far more on collective perceptions — ways of thought — than on techniques.

If a machine's motor makes an odd noise and if the supervisor says to the machinist, "Oh, don't worry. This machine has always run like that," or "This isn't your problem. Let the technicians handle it," the machinist ceases to regard the noise as an anomaly. Similarly, a newly hired worker who expresses concern about defective items arriving from a supplier quickly readjusts her own quality standard to the one prevailing in the

---

[4] Chapter 7 will reexamine achieving progress by improving current resources.

firm if the reply is, "Oh, that's normal. We've had problems like that for years."

For valid observations to emerge, events must be approached as phenomena outside a blame-attributing context.

Lastly, the factor that produces effective observers is the capability of the observers to act upon whatever they observe. Thus any responsibility to observe should be associated with the responsibility to seek progress. Involving employees in visual observation requires careful preparation.

Visual observation includes these four phases:

- Displaying standards
- Developing a response system
- Recording problems
- Seeing further

The fourth phase is derived from the principle that to see events occurring around oneself is not enough to observe reality. Often one must become aware of circumstances outside one's own territory.

DISPLAYING STANDARDS

Chapter 3 emphasized the essential role of methodological standards. In reference to work instructions, we encountered such expressions as "Our Bible," "A road map," or "A starting point for achieving improvement." Those standards, pertaining to know-how, were perceived from the standpoint of the actor, the operator.

The standards we will discuss here are useful to an observer as well as an actor. They enable an observer to understand the condition of the operating system: machines, products, positioning of various items, and so on. The function of standards is to facilitate interpretation of the visible field, and, more specifically, to allow recognition of anomalies that may demand responses.[5]

These points of reference are not indispensable in extremely hierarchical organizations, where executives are the only people entrusted with interpretation of visible reality. These points become indispensable, however, when a company desires participation by the greatest possible number.

When a company adopts the principle of the systematic display of standards, visual communication helps develop a collective observation system. The objective is to provide the entire community with a sole cipher for interpreting its environment.

Instead of saying, "This area is really a mess," for example, take photographs when the area is spotless. Instead of saying, "Everything is out of order," mark designated areas on the floor with colored lines, so that everyone can understand the expression "an orderly work area." (This concept is not as obvious as we may believe, because each person's concept of order is unique.)

Instead of saying, "You've still left parts on the floor," provide bins whose standard function is storage of misplaced parts. (Figure 5-2) Instead of saying, "Watch the needle closely. If it goes too high, call me," provide a set of templates with red and green standard areas, and mount the discs on a dial according to processes occurring at specific times. (Figure 5-3) Indicate the proper response in the event of malfunctions, with a list of telephone numbers of people who must be contacted.

---

[5] According to the Japan Management Association: "A *visual control* provides a visible standard so that anyone can tell at a glance whether an abnormality has occurred. (*Canon Production System* (Cambridge, Mass.: Productivity Press, 1987), p. 12.) This definition incorporates three vital points: Standards must be visible; anomalies must be visible; and anyone should be able to adopt the role of an observer.

Figure 5-2. The Facom plant in Nevers, France. A small bin installed in the work area collects miscellaneous parts. The text above the bin reads: "Zero Mistakes — Let's Put an End to Mix-ups! Put any parts you find on the floor into this bin, as well as any items that do not correspond to current production runs."

DEVELOPING A RESPONSE SYSTEM

In designing visual response systems, uphold three principles:

- Transmit prompt feedback.
- Place messages close at hand.
- Ensure information-sharing within the group.

In the first instance, responding promptly means preventing a problem from persisting. Because automatic machines are proliferating, continuous monitoring by the operator has become difficult. When a machine is improperly positioned, the severity of the damage can depend upon how quickly intervention occurs.

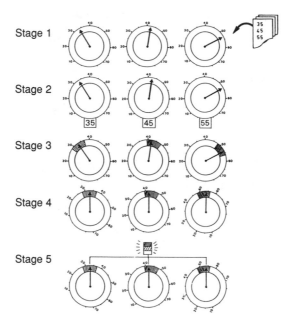

(1) Standard values are entered on a sheet which is apart from the dials.

(2) Standard values are indicated on dials.

(3) Standard values are indicated in color on the respective instrument, although each dial must be separately monitored.

(4) One can compare to standard values with a mere glance, even from a distance.

(5) When one of the instruments deviates from the standard, an alarm signal is activated. This final form of control is the level that should precede introduction of automatic control.

Figure 5-3. Five stages of progress toward visual control (according to Ryuji Fukuda).

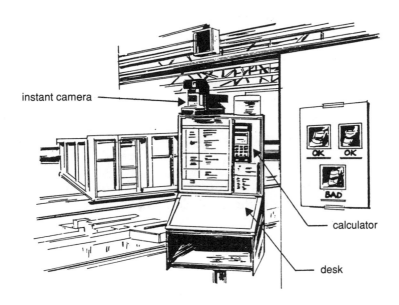

instant camera

calculator

desk

**Figure 5-4. Snapshots are used extensively at the Valeo plant near
Le Mans.** They simultaneously allow definition of standards, as indicated in
the illustration, as well as documenting anomalies. This is one of the basic
tools for visual inspection.

Placing messages close at hand allows fundamental problems to be solved. The probability of discovering actual causes for events decreases extremely quickly between the time a problem occurs and an analysis is undertaken. Two weeks after the fact, no one recalls the precise circumstances, which hinders reconstruction of the context or comprehension of causes. A detective who arrives at the scene three months after the crime would be relatively unsuccessful in finding clues and reliable witnesses.

Last, keeping all employees informed about events occurring in the workplace offers two advantages. The first is an increased ability to intervene — the closest people are able to respond. The second advantage is of an attitudinal nature.

Something more than mere information is in operation when everyone can see the way the group responds to events:

- Defective items are clearly designated as such and it is possible to immediately stop a faulty machine.
- Machines with oil leaks are shut down immediately.
- Parts lying on the floor are picked up.
- Suppliers of defective components are required to come to the plant to explain.

The company's system of values is being molded even more effectively than by the most eloquent speeches.

Quality at the Source: An Example

A motor vehicle assembly line like the one at Renault's plant in Sandouville is organized in a particularly rigid way, which is ill-suited for modifying the assembly workers' ways of performing tasks. As a result, the transformation introduced under the heading "quality at the source" is even more interesting.

Until recently, when an assembly worker failed to mount a given part correctly, the instruction was to leave the automobile as it was. Teams whose function was to remedy defects were situated at intervals of about one hundred meters, so that vehicles could continue along the assembly line. Members of these teams lost significant amounts of time. First they had to locate the defects. Corrective work was often more burdensome because the initial defect had prevented proper assembly of other parts.

"In the beginning," a manager stated, "newly hired workers used to tell their supervisors when they couldn't install a part. The reply was: 'Don't knock yourself out. That's the retouchers' job.' Then the new people would avoid any special effort to improve matters because there was no reason to push the retouchers out of a job."

Today, the line is equipped with an alarm system. When an assembly worker encounters difficulties, he or she uses the alarm. (Figure 5-5) The position number lights up on a board (Figure 5-6), and a technical aide comes to help. The goal is for each vehicle to be processed correctly as it is assembled.

The "quality at the source" method may appear to be common sense. Nevertheless, it has profoundly changed the workers' habits.

Figure 5-5. The Renault plant in Sandouville. Pulling the cord sends a signal in case of problems.

- All possible measures are adopted to ensure that vehicles are properly assembled from the start.
- In the event of a problem, each member of the team is informed by a flashing signal. One can see whether the process is occurring properly, and if difficulties have arisen. Everyone is aware of how the production unit is functioning as a whole.
- The production team's efforts not only remedy problems but record its actions so development of permanent solutions can occur. (Figure 5-11)

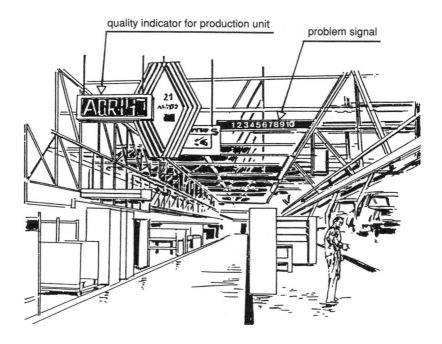

Figure 5-6. The Renault plant in Sandouville. The problem-signaling system.

- Last, the existence of the system itself is a message. Observing the lights turning on provides recognition that something has changed in relation to the previous method. At Sandouville, everyone knows that "doing the job" is not enough now; it must also be done well.

Highway Breakdowns

Introducing this kind of system is not merely a technical procedure. A new system also represents a change in ways of thinking. That is why preparations for a project of this kind are so important. The initial steps are necessarily collective, and the entire production team must participate.

At Sandouville, a pilot unit tested the "quality at the source" method in a trial area. Later, it was easier to introduce the project throughout the assembly line.

A working group consisting of machinists and technicians met several times until the project was fully developed. Lively discussions occurred. At one point, there was a proposal for combining the signal light with an audible alarm, but a machinist objected: "Imagine all these buzzers going off in our work area. That's going to be a damned distraction!" Another member of the group replied, "That will bother us far less than people having breakdowns out on the expressway because of assembly defects."

Information Returning Upstream

The principle of quality at the source means that only acceptable items travel through the plant. For technical reasons, achieving this goal is not always possible. At times, machining defects occur that are only detectable during the assembly process, or parts are improperly assembled that are only detectable by testing.

Nevertheless, the purpose of displaying results is the same: to make information available as soon as possible at the location where the procedures are taking place, and to display this information so that it will be visible to everyone. (Figure 5-7)

Talking Machines

The Sandouville assembly line's display system allows centralization of data from more than ten work stations. Other instances employ simpler methods, including three-color lights placed on each machine. (Figure 5-8) The Japanese name for these lights is *andon*, which means "lantern." Kiyoshi Suzaki points out that the purpose of a lantern is to guide a person

Figure 5-7. The Renault plant at Sandouville. On the assembly line, a detailed inspection of a car taken from the end of the line measures quality on a regular basis. Every two hours, an employee records on a board data about cars produced by the 20-person assembly section. Thus each assembly worker knows immediately whether the unit is performing acceptable work.

Figure 5-8. The Solex plant at Evreux. The arrow points to an illuminated signal above a work station.

along the path by illuminating difficulties.[6] This poetic description evokes the intention of facilitating the supervision of production units by everyone who works in them.

The concept of collective monitoring of work areas emerged recently. In some plants, the equation of one operator to one machine prevails. This equation was valid in the era of manual labor, but it is no longer valid in the era of automation. The system of operator-machine communication must allow more effective and less costly monitoring.

Alain Hue, an assistant to the manager of the production department at Renault's Sandouville plant, provides a vivid description of the advantages that an effective system of communication between human beings and machines offers.

> I recently learned about the exact nature of this phenomenon when a malfunction kept my office telephone from ringing. I was able to talk on my phone, but there was no way for me to be alerted by an audible signal. At one moment, I was waiting for an important call. Because I knew that the telephone wouldn't ring, I was immobilized. I had to pick up the receiver from time to time to see if anyone was on the other end of the line.
>
> I thought of certain items of equipment where the operator has very little to do for most of the time. Performing certain steps from time to time is sufficient, tending the machine when it has a problem, resupplying it, or changing a tool. Although machines have become more technically advanced, the system of communicating with human beings is still unsuitable. The system obliges the operator to remain present to monitor the operation of a given machine, just like my telephone that couldn't ring.

6 Kiyoshi Suzaki, "In the process of challenge, and the use of the Jidoka concept," *Review of the Association for Manufacturing Excellence (AME)*, Spring, 1988.

Jidohka – A New Martial Art?

Andon lights and the "quality at the source" procedure are aspects of the system the Japanese call *jidohka*, or "autonomation" or "automation with a human touch." The concept is sometimes misunderstood as merely a reacting to anomalies in a given process, or just an automatic machine that inspects the products it manufactures.

In reality, jidohka depends on devices activated either by people or by automatic machinery to obtain responses in the event of problems. According to Kiyoshi Suzaki, introducing a jidohka system involves creating conditions for increased autonomy for production systems.[7]

Suzaki emphasizes that the autonomy associated with jidohka is much broader than its English-language equivalents might lead us to assume. Production units gain a mode of organization that allows not only proper responses to problems, but the development of preventive measures — autonomously — for eliminating recurrences. In other words, making the machine stop automatically does not make jidohka. Employees must analyze phenomena and seek reasons for problems, with the goal of finding permanent solutions.

A general approach to autonomy, not only for processes but for progress, jidohka is both a self-control system and a self-organization method. As Suzaki says: "Jidohka is an exercise for building the muscles and nerves of production." Thus, jidohka is akin to a martial art for factories.

A Few More Dollars

The American firm Granville Phillips, which manufactures electronic equipment, discovered an imaginative way to convey the message that there are positive sides to problems.

---

[7] Suzaki, *AME Review*, op. cit.

Three-colored signal lights were installed at the assembly locations for electronic circuits. The workers could turn on these andon lights when they encountered difficulties with parts or equipment.

When the lights were installed, the manager observed that employees were reluctant to activate the signal. The employees hardly ever used the lights for fear of disturbing someone. Their unconscious fear was the watchword of the past: Do not make waves, do not stop work.

The manager arrived at the idea of attaching a sticker with a dollar sign to each light. The message was clear. Notwithstanding disruptions caused by suspension of work, these situations represent opportunities to earn dollars, assuming that it is possible to find definitive solutions that prevent problems from recurring.

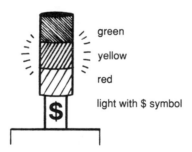

Figure 5-9. An innovative illuminated signal.

Taking Action before Accidents Occur

Some firms have adopted the objective of intervening before problems arise. The earliest signs that may foreshadow an accident are called *warusa-kagen* in Japanese. This expression refers to anomalies that do not prevent completion of work, but their detection allows prevention of breakdowns and improved understanding of how the equipment functions.

Figure 5-10. The Reydel plant in Gondecourt. The injection unit is equipped with a communication system that allows direct notification of the repairs department when a problem develops. A message is run on an illuminated electronic board explaining the type of malfunction, location, and reason for shutting down the machine. This panel is not intended solely for the repair staff, but also to make everyone in the work area more aware of problems affecting machinery. Thus, a worker whose machine is malfunctioning may feel less isolated. The problem is also his or her coworkers' problem.

In the presence of anomalies that are not overly serious, we often continue as long as conditions allow. This attitude is similar to the response of a driver who hears a strange noise in the car's motor, but waits for a breakdown before responding. Every anomaly is an interesting sign that may allow avoidance of more serious difficulties.

Masaaki Imai describes a production unit at the Tokai Rika plant in Japan, where machinists are encouraged to report all of these warusa-kagen or "quasi-problems." To boost the detection campaign, management decided to regard the number of these warnings-at-no-cost as an indicator of the employees' observation capabilities. Within one year the plant recorded 534 situations that, if not identified beforehand, would have led to serious consequences in terms of its output or equipment.[8]

RECORDING PROBLEMS

When the Renault team at Sandouville prepared the "quality at the source" project, it provided a way for problems to be recorded and analyzed. Thus, the team placed a chart near the assembly line. (Figure 5-11) Every defect was noted on this chart, and defects were classified by origin in the form of a diagram.

According to one executive, the outcome was extremely favorable. Systematic analysis identified the principal causes of defects and allowed the adoption of corrective measures. Within a few weeks, the number of defective items declined so sharply that it became possible to eliminate corrective work. Workers who performed retouching tasks were assigned to more constructive functions, such as technical assistance and training of machinists.

Practical Recommendations

To maintain record-keeping and save time, design data-entry documents to achieve maximum reduction of the workload. Creating an input document with a predetermined form offers several advantages. First, the time required to enter data can be reduced. Use preselected symbols: magnetic disks, colors, and so on. Second, the act of creating group designations for defects (and of showing actual part defects in a physical form near the charts, as Citroën has done, Figure 5-14) permits

---

[8] Imai, *Kaizen*, op. cit., p. 165.

Figure 5-11. The Renault plant in Sandouville. A chart for analyzing problems is situated near the assembly line.

Figure 5-12. The Favi plant in Hallencourt. Statistical process control (SPC) uses graphs to record measurements of products as machine processing is completed. Monitoring allows intervention before departures from acceptable tolerances occur. Variations can be interpreted to understand the particular process better. SPC depends on active participation by machinists. The results are excellent if this method is applied under suitable conditions.

designation in a practical way. This condition is indispensable if problems are to be solved independently of any kind of fault-finding context.

Another advantage is the establishment of a complete list of possible defects. Classifying them by using Pareto diagrams can motivate the people responsible for entering data because they participate directly in analyzing it.

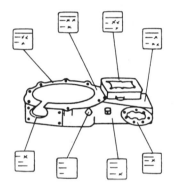

Figure 5-13. A defect location diagram. Whenever the occasion allows, it is advantageous to accompany the design documents with diagrams or photographs of the product that show the locations of the most common defects. It is sufficient to mark X's in the appropriate areas.

Some firms prefer to record problems in a log. This approach requires less space and facilitates subsequent use. Nevertheless, a large chart visible to everyone is preferable, even if it is necessary to record overall figures in a log later.

Precise measurements are not always required. To record shutdowns for a machine, for example, it is sufficient to measure the precise duration of shutdowns exceeding fifteen minutes.

Other shutdowns can be simply indicated by marks within columns of a chart. The limited duration of these shutdowns and their effect on statistics means that the measure of their frequency is sufficient to indicate their effect on shutdown time.

Last, an instant camera should be used to define quality standards. Because nothing matches the impact of photographs, also use them for recording interesting phenomena. A defective part, a damaged pallet, a malfunctioning system are all indications that should be captured in their original form. Photographs can be attached to sheets that describe problems, or they can be magnetically mounted on the chart used to record data. A twofold advantage ensues. Photographs capture the attention of passersby. Photographs also increase the likelihood of understanding the phenomena that are being observed.

Maintaining Contact

The act of recording data does not eliminate the need for daily contact in a team. Some information concerning processes

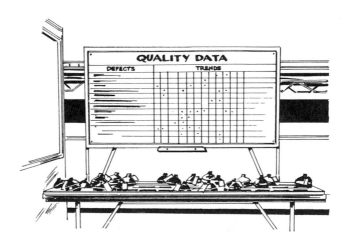

Figure 5-14. The Citroën plant in Caen. A large chart is posted within the work area to allow recording and analysis of quality problems. The parts on the display stand represent different types of defects, with each defect labeled. With this mode of presentation, anyone can easily identify defects and record figures on the chart. Moreover, everyone passing by the chart can understand the precise nature of difficulties that the team may be encountering.

cannot be explicitly described using visual methods, and must therefore be exchanged by word of mouth. Workers can save time by not recording everything in writing, although in this instance frequent contact is necessary.

At its Gondecourt plant, the J. Reydel company introduced the "quality minute" principle. The entire team halts its work for one minute per hour. During this pause, everyone cites the phenomena observed at his or her work station. Observations considered interesting are recorded in the team's log, and they are discussed in a later meeting.

At the Physio-Control plant in Seattle, regular meetings occur at the team level to discuss problems encountered during the day.

A chart is positioned at the beginning of each assembly line (Figure 5-15), and team members who have encountered any problems record brief descriptions of the events on this chart. Employees use felt-tipped pens of different colors, according to the nature of the problem (equipment, processes, materials), to facilitate use of data. At the end of each meeting, problems that require monitoring are recorded in a log.

"We used to have a lot of minor problems throughout the work day. They weren't very serious, and we never recorded them," a worker in the assembly section stated. "We couldn't be bothering the team leader every minute, and, by the end of the day, we had often forgotten about the situation. Now, it's become a reflex. Whenever we observe a problem of any kind — improperly sorted parts, problems with tooling, incomplete files — we record it on the chart. That way, we're sure that problems won't be overlooked."

Seeing Further

Seeing reality means observing and interpreting one's environment. In some instances, however, one must also understand how events unfold at locations both upstream and downstream

Figure 5-15. The Physio-Control plant in Seattle. A board for recording problems. The small red flag at the top of the board has a specific function. When a serious problem cannot be resolved promptly, a member of the group raises the flag. Thus, everyone — other teams, technicians, management — is aware that the team has encountered a critical problem that will require special attention and assistance from everyone.

from one's own. The visible environment acquires a broader meaning. Seeing reality also means seeing further.

This idea had probably entered the mind of the purchasing manager in a large distillery of cognac. "On several occasions, we had problems with labels for our bottles, because labels were being improperly cut out at the supplier's production location," he explained. "In spite of the recommendations in our specifications, the press operator was piling too many sheets on the press. Whenever it happened, we informed the printer's sales division. A few weeks later, after sending letters back and forth and wasting time in several unproductive meetings, we finally obtained a commitment in principle, although there was no observable improvement."

Chronic recurrence of difficulties finally induced the firm to abandon traditional communications channels. "We became doubtful," the purchasing manager explained, "that the worker who was producing labels with the cutter had been made aware of the difficulties arising from a lack of consistency in operating procedures. Did we have to keep communicating through the usual channels, or could we make direct contact with this worker?

"We decided to do a videotape," the manager explained. "It's twelve minutes long. Our video production techniques were simple, and the budget was very low. This videotape shows very precisely what happens on our packaging line when labels are poorly cut. The feed system jams, glue begins to overflow, and the line must shut down for us to remove bunches of crumpled labels.

"This was the first time," he added, "that it was possible for the worker who produced labels to see the disaster. In the past, the worker had merely received recommendations from the supervisor, who had been notified by the production manager, who had been informed by the sales manager. There's no longer a need to give long explanations or to reprimand anyone. Seeing's enough, in order to understand."

According to the purchasing manager, the results were surprising. "Not only was there a fast improvement in quality, but we were shocked to receive suggestions from some of the supplier's employees who wanted to propose ways of making our manufacturing process more efficient once they had seen it on film! Because this venture was so successful, we produced other videotapes. Today, there is a videotape for each category of products that we buy."

The Current Flows

Opening a plant to its external environment in this way requires a profound transformation of attitudes. For years, production units existed in sealed compartments, focused inward.

Machinists, team leaders, and engineers rarely left their own areas, and few direct links were maintained with the world outside. Executives and their operating departments had a monopoly on external contact. Compartmentalization was a result of prevailing organizational concepts.

Today the situation is changing. The need to advance and to mobilize the entire work force for meeting the challenges of international competition are battering down the partitions. Clients and suppliers come into factories and communicate directly with their counterparts. Members of production teams visit clients' facilities in order to see how the products they manufacture are used. Long-standing taboos are giving way to the only imperative that matters: better production.

As subsequent examples demonstrate, most companies that open their production units this way have extremely favorable results. One point is clear: For the current to flow, you need only establish the circuit.

CONTACT WITH SUPPLIERS

A firm's suppliers are often strangers to its production units. Their remoteness can be measured not only in miles but in time. The supplier's schedule is open at Week 36 when a plant calls the supplier during Week 22. When a plant is evaluating the quality of material produced in February, the supplier is preparing goods intended for May. If suppliers and users must live in worlds separated by a quarter of a year, how can they arrive at shared viewpoints?

Firms that have selected just-in-time methods have found it necessary to modify extensively their systems of relationships with suppliers. When extra inventory is no longer there in the event of a production problem, suppliers' production units and clients' production units must be in direct contact, without hindrances. Prompt responses and development of effective solutions for every problem are vital.

Communication is changing. Necessary information can no longer be transmitted solely by purchasing and sales departments. Cooperation based on frequent workplace-to-workplace contact is emerging: The goal is to confront problems without delays, at the levels where there is the greatest possibility of achieving solutions.

When the NUMMI plant changed management and adopted Toyota as its model, suppliers were invited to the production areas much more often. In the past, there were limited opportunities to visit the plant.

According to the quality manager at LTV Steel, which supplies the NUMMI plant, these visits allow key topics to be approached directly, and information and feedback can be received firsthand. They also give a better understanding of the client's outlook than lengthy explanations offer.

Contact is not limited to executives. More than 30 machinists have visited Fremont during the past year. "Initially, there were some problems with rolls of steel being rejected," said the quality manager. "These problems were resolved so quickly because we were constantly receiving rapid, accurate, and reliable information, which never passed through intermediaries."

The results of LTV Steel's contact with its client's production teams are directly visible. At the rear of the stamping area, where rolls of steel are waiting to be placed upon the presses, one sees a large board that measures six feet by nine feet. (Figure 5-16)

Samples of sheet steel are mounted on this board, which was prepared by LTV Steel. Each sheet, which measures approximately 30 centimeters along the side, indicates a sample defect in the material. The name of the defect is written below.

"I had this board installed," the quality manager said, "so that our client's production teams could speak our language. In the event of problems, communication is easier this way." The board prepared by LTV Steel also includes texts and photographs that explain the process of steel production. "Because of these explanations," he added, "members of NUMMI's teams

Figure 5-16. The NUMMI plant, Fremont, California. A board installed in the stamping area to explain the supplier's manufacturing process and the principal defects that may occur.

can better understand the relationships between steel production as LTV Steel does it and the stamping process that they are responsible for."

A Place to Meet the Supplier

When the Renault plant at Sandouville sought to strengthen direct contact with suppliers, a decision to establish meeting places in its work areas was adopted. (Figure 5-17) The purpose was for suppliers to come to the plant and become directly involved in solving the various problems that production units had encountered with the goods being supplied.

The meeting place is an office located near the assembly line. The supplier's records are available here. Outside the office hangs a schedule for weekly meetings and a chart summarizing problems with all suppliers. "When suppliers come here," a unit supervisor said, "they look at the chart. If I see a supplier turn-ing pale, it's usually because she has just realized that her com-petitor is in the green area, while she still has a fair number of red disks." (See the chart in Figure 7-4.)

Initially, suppliers came to Sandouville only when prob-lems arose. Now they visit the plant periodically to maintain contact. A member of the assembly department who is responsi-ble for coordination with the purchasing department presides over the meetings. The unit supervisor also attends these meet-ings. When the discussion turns to practical problems, the entire group visits the assembly line to ask machinists their opinions.

As did LTV Steel, other suppliers have produced films, so employees can look at television sets in their units to see how suppliers' plants function and to know about suppliers' efforts in terms of quality and organization.

"Formerly, people on the line were completely isolated," explained an employee responsible for promoting relations with

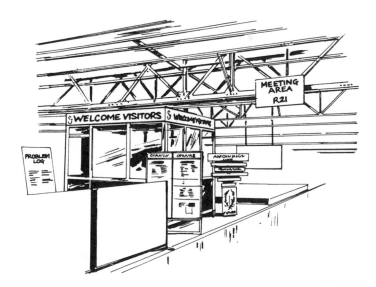

Figure 5-17. The Renault plant in Sandouville. An area for meeting with suppliers.

suppliers. "Now, if there's a problem with a product we've bought, we can call the unit that has manufactured our parts directly. If the person whom we contact has any questions about our problem, we can say: 'Come over and take a look, because these are your parts. Maybe you'll be able to assemble them, because we can't find a way to do it.'"

"Since the new system was introduced," she continued, "I've seen definite improvement in quality among our suppliers. They pay much more attention to what we tell them."

The suppliers are justified in heeding the assembly teams' observations. As a Renault supplier confided, "Imagine the situation. You've been summoned to the assembly line because of a quality problem. You're surrounded by work stations that install your products. Under these conditions, it's difficult, even for an excellent salesperson, to deny the problem or shrug it off. It's difficult to try to sweeten the pill by mentioning tight schedules, the condition of the market, or prices for next year. The defect is right before your eyes. People can't do their work properly, and that's the only thing that matters."

CONTACT WITH CLIENTS

Professor Robert Millen of Northeastern University in Boston, Massachusetts, relates the following incident. It indicates the distinctive nature of the relationships that arise when production personnel meet the people who use the products.

Imagine an aircraft plant in southern England, during World War II. Workers leaning into the cockpits are assembling Spitfire fighters to be sent into combat within a few weeks. A group of visitors advances from the other end of the work area. The workers, concentrating upon the delicate assembly process, pursue their tasks without being distracted. In the past months, there have been so many visits from the Ministry. Generals adorned with ribbons and medals, along with curious bureaucrats, are coming to ensure that production is running smoothly, that rules are being upheld, and that Britain is being defended. In the assembly unit, no one raises his head.

Suddenly, a commotion is heard at the end of the aisle. Shouts and "hurrahs" resound through the frigid work area. The group draws closer to the workers. They hear a buzz of voices. The visitors are four fighter pilots, wearing their flight suits.

The pilots describe the beginning of a mission to the workers — humming motor, and an airplane climbs smoothly into the mist at daybreak. The workers listen, frozen with emotion, their tools in their hands. The pilots describe dogfights in the air, the fuel tanks that must be jettisoned, their blind trust in the roaring engines, their hands gripping the controls, and the airplane lurching. They describe chases, feints, dives, and their relief at returning to their bases at dusk.

What are the pilots saying to the workers? "Thank you. Thank you for producing such good airplanes, and thanks again, because without your close attention, we may not have been here to express our thanks."

Learning from Supermarkets

Rather than aircraft, Fleury Michon produces prepackaged meat products and cooked items. Nevertheless, the firm's executives must have concluded that there are always "pilots" at the end of the line — namely, consumers of the firm's products — and that it was important for production personnel to meet these consumers. "Strangely, when we took our employees to see our products in supermarkets, they became extremely critical," said Mr. Petit, the communications manager. "Organizing direct contact between employees and customers is extremely beneficial. Finding themselves in the consumer's position gave workers a much clearer concept of quality.

"A minor defect, a crooked label, a product poorly positioned inside the package, or other defects that might have seemed acceptable in the workplace became truly unbearable when they were observed in the case next to competitors' products."

Fleury Michon created a communication strategy with the aim of promoting contact between production personnel and consumers. The motto is, "People must become directly aware; they must see things with their own eyes."

Employees from the shipping department and sales personnel visited supermarkets. Upon returning, they described to their coworkers the arrival of a 20-ton shipment in a congested delivery area, high-speed unloading procedures, storing of packages, and the administrative process for packing lists and invoices. "Now we understand why our clients are so demanding about certain things that seem to be mere details!" they concluded.

To upgrade its system for promoting contact between production and the market, Fleury Michon periodically offers its sales force one-week training periods at the plant. During training periods, sales representatives visit work areas, enter into discussions with production employees, and seek explanations about ways in which products are being manufactured, as well as ask questions about new equipment. Each executive must explain his or her section's activities, and indicate anticipated improvements.

"This is an especially profitable exercise," the human relations manager confirmed. "If the person responsible for giving an explanation to the sales representatives suggests that the slicing machine's programmable control system will be replaced by a new microcomputer, he's risking disaster. The audience expects to hear how the plant will try to reduce delivery periods, improve quality assurance, and develop new products more quickly. In a situation where audience interest has to be maintained, our speakers must quickly determine clients' true concerns."

From Producer to Consumer

Buying a luxury automobile is, to a certain extent, buying a portion of the factory. That is what Renault's executives thought when they invited buyers to pick up their cars at the plant in the presence of a Renault sales manager.

Before taking possession of their cars, buyers are allowed to visit production areas to see how cars are assembled and to speak with the workers. Then each buyer is proudly guided toward the car, whose registration plate bears the name of the worker who performed the final adjustments and inspection.

Contact between the production and sales sectors is also made directly when new models are placed on the market. When the R21 turbo model was introduced, a group of twelve highly skilled workers from the retouching section – who were available because of improvements in quality at the end of the line — spent three months visiting the sales network. Their role was to establish contact with customers, and, returning to the plant on Fridays, to report on customers' observations about quality.

According to Raymond Savoye, the plant manager, this project offered many lessons: "Before launching this project, people said, 'Watch out! It's essential to avoid bringing your workers into contact with customers! They may say anything under the sun!' What happened? Our customers' responses were excellent. Direct contact with the people who produced their cars offered them additional assurance that problems would be given proper attention."

On the Deck

According to the manager of a furniture factory, placing production personnel in direct contact with the realities of the market generates enthusiasm and motivation: "Imagine when people who spend all of their time working in a ship's engine room go on deck for the first time and discover the sky and islands."

"During a show in Paris we were exhibiting our furniture," the manager explained. "I asked four workers to participate in the activities of a sales team assigned to our booth. My intention was to give them an opportunity to talk with customers, to listen to their questions, and to understand their concerns."

"The results were favorable," the manager said.

> First, I found that some of our employees had unrecognized talents, and that, with additional training, they would be excellent in sales. Moreover, I was astounded to see their strictness in regard to quality. When a sales representative praised one woman for the quality of her work, she replied, "It's not really perfect; we could have done much better." Then, in response to the sales representative's astonished look, she pointed out a minute defect in a piece of furniture. A client without extremely sharp eyes would have been incapable of detecting this defect.
>
> If she had been criticized about quality by the sales representative, she would never have referred to this minor imperfection as a defect. She probably would have replied, "It's nothing at all." The fact that she was complimented encouraged her to present herself as much more demanding.
>
> After the show, when the workers returned to the plant, they described everything to their coworkers. Winning portions of the market, advertising budgets, giving priority to customer service, zero defects — these were their own words now.

RETURNING TO THE SOURCE

These examples point to the benefits of contact between production teams and suppliers or clients. Below is an excerpt from a lecture given at the Ecole Supérieure d'Electricité in Paris by Raymond Savoye, the manager of the Renault plant in Sandouville. Savoye explains an innovative way to promote contact between executives and production personnel within the same company.

For years, we knew that the work station was the critical point for quality and prices. For years, people said things were not going well. But many people talk at length about a situation without having firsthand knowledge of the facts. They tend to remain on the level of general observations.

You know the story. Manufacturing says, "It's the maintenance department; they've fouled things up again." The quality department says, "Oh, those suppliers — they'll do just about anything!" At Sandouville, we needed a way out of this system. We found our target in start-up situations — when new models are introduced and the entire company is mobilized. That's where our executives have direct contact with real problems. They really had a grasp of the process, but that was just a one-shot thing; it wasn't a permanent system.

We began to seek a real solution. One day, my assistant manager, Mr. Marchand, came out of a meeting and said, "I think I've discovered what we should do. Next September, I'm going to put on overalls and go on the assembly line. I'm going to set an example: all of our executives will have to work in production units on a regular basis."

The idea had come to him after a meeting with the Club Méditerranée in the course of an exchange of quality-improvement plans. The Club Méditerranée's training director told us that he becomes a village "chief" again once each year. "I'm the one who must coordinate the evening for all village members, and if necessary, bring the food to them at their tables."

This is what led us to announce to the entire staff (all employees except for the line workers) that they would be asked to spend three days a year as an assembly line worker. Then, to drive home the point, Mr. Marchand described his experience, and this was extremely interesting. He received an excellent welcome from the workers, and he gained an understanding of numerous concrete points: the screwing machine that is too far away, the set of tools that do not fit properly, the part that is difficult to install, and so on.

Since that point, more than 400 people, starting with top management, have rolled up their sleeves to work in the production units. Mr. Garsmeur, the operations manager at corporate headquarters, came to Sandouville and later sent me a short note that said, "I'll be back. This is incredible." The head of the research unit for automobile bodies is at Sandouville, and he'll go on the line today. People from our foreign sales department were here yesterday. When they saw what we've done, they said, "We'll be coming to Sandouville."

It's important not to be afraid. Someone from the corporate offices was a bit dazed and anxious to know what would happen on the factory floor. "I won't be able to keep up the pace!" The workers replied, "It's a good thing you can't keep up the pace, because if you could it would mean that our jobs are too easy."

This project — *Returning to the Source* — is readily accepted by our employees because we made an effort to communicate — first to explain the project and then to explain the results. Close attention is needed, however, because the whole project is a long march. If we had proposed it in this form two years ago, without any introduction, it would have been a fiasco.

This project has rubbed some people the wrong way. We've been told that it is a little "Maoist." Yet the project has altered the level of awareness for many of us much more effectively than lectures. We're no longer satisfied with just talking about things.

6

Process Indicators

A text about management gave one manager the idea to display performance indicators in work areas. The book read: "How can you expect your employees to be interested in what they are doing if they are not informed of the results? Can you imagine a football team discussing its games without knowing the score?"

The idea of announcing the score pleased the manager greatly. He summoned the head of his administrative department, and together they defined several interesting indicators. The necessary computations would not pose any problems: All of the data was already in the computer. Moreover, with the small amount of effort required to prepare a simple program, it would be possible to produce graphs directly from the printer. Shortly thereafter, a display case adorned with a gilded frame appeared in the work area. Everyone acknowledged that it produced a favorable impression by enhancing the decor of a fairly austere milieu. The manager, extremely proud, never passed up an opportunity to show visitors this tangible evidence of his new policy of openness: "The entire firm is being mobilized to improve quality and efficiency," he explained. "Monitoring performance is no longer reserved for management. Now it's everybody's concern."

Three months later, the manager observed that inside the glass case the charts were out of date by two weeks. When the head of the administrative department was consulted, he replied that he was no longer receiving figures he needed. "In any case," he explained with a disillusioned air, "I think we're on the wrong track. At first, people expressed curiosity about the production curves. Everything was new and attractive. Now they walk by without even glancing at it. Why should so much effort be made to supply information to people who aren't interested? Remember, it was the same story with the company newsletter. Five hundred copies on glossy paper, and most of them ended up in the trash can."

The manager's idea of a football team and a score was not erroneous. The manager had merely forgotten one point. When a player looks at the scoreboard, he would never think to say: "Seven to nothing! Good grief! Our poor coach will have plenty to complain about. But as far as I'm concerned, I think I played OK this time."

If football teams allot so much importance to the score, they do so because they are fully involved in the game. A team regards the results as representing *its* efforts, *its* skill, and *its* progress. Managers in a plant may be tempted to display indicators in work areas, but what is the value of doing so if the team is not concerned with its performance?

This problem has already been encountered in relation to the display of work instructions or production schedules. Success depends on a process in which information is owned. With indicators, we have to anticipate a rather difficult process.

Indeed, for years analytical accounting and management control have been applied in an overly centralized way. Figures defined in offices without consulting the work areas flowed back to the offices receiving no data in return. The prevalent opinion in production units was: "Management uses performance measurements to see whether we're working hard or not." Charts acquired a moral connotation. The hidden meaning was: *The reason for performing measurements is to judge us.*

Given an unfavorable context, we must define the objectives of a project at the outset. Formerly, indicators maintained control over production units. Today, indicators offer opportunities to motivate employees. Thus, an error is perpetuated. Indicators displayed in work areas should have only one purpose: to become tools for production teams, exactly as machines, robots, or material-handling equipment.

PROCESS INDICATORS

A few years ago, when one watched a football game on television, the only indicator provided was the score. Today, the announcers indicate the total number of successful or unsuccessful attempts to score, the amount of time spent in the other team's zone, the average amount of time for a given team to retain possession of the ball, the average number of passes by individual teams, and much more.

A score is a *results indicator*. Other parameters are *process indicators*. The same distinction exists in factories. Output levels are results indicators. The way that a factory fulfills this role can be assessed with process indicators: numbers of malfunctions and rejections, quality levels for raw materials, regularity of resupplying, average volumes of work-in-process, and so on.

In *Kaizen*, Masaaki Imai demonstrates that Western firms have always given priority to results indicators, whereas Japanese firms have developed process indicators far more extensively. According to Imai, this difference originates from two distinct management styles. Westerners are more keenly interested in short-term benefits, but they allot limited significance to ways of obtaining them. On the other hand, the Japanese believe that defining appropriate methods and following them deserves priority.[1] To recast Imai's idea, Westerners count the golden eggs, whereas the Japanese pay more attention to the health of the goose.

---

[1] Imai, *Kaizen*, op. cit. at 16-21.

Hence, the new types of indicators are indicators that determine whether processes obey certain rules. A large variety of information can be displayed. Production units are not confined to measuring scores — the production level. They can also measure factors in the game: reliability of equipment, employees' mobility, numbers of small improvements, production lead times, and so on. Results indicators are not ignored, but they are no longer viewed in isolation from ways of pursuing them. Inherently valid results do not exist. Everything depends on the path followed.

A Manufacturing Perspective

Process indicators allow recognition of ways of achieving results, with the underlying concept that valid methods must have been followed before congratulating oneself for a high-quality performance.

One question arises immediately. What does a "valid method" mean? How can process indicators be defined if one has not determined what constitutes a valid process?

Why should production lead time be measured if no one is convinced of a need to reduce it? Why should rejection rates be studied if there is no soundly developed policy in regard to quality? Why waste time monitoring suppliers' delivery times if a plant is protected from delays by maintaining large inventories? Why should time for changing dies be analyzed, or employees' multiple abilities be indicated if a firm's management does not have a carefully developed concept for the flexible use of its production resources?

A firm that lacks a precise manufacturing strategy will find few process indicators that it must display. Until the 1980s, it was possible for western manufacturing goals — production with saturation of capacity — to emphasize indicators minimally. When one is driving a car at maximum speed, one has little inclination to examine the instrument panel.

Our industrial perspectives attained a more advanced level of awareness only with the appearance of such policies as total quality, just-in-time, optimum service, and preventing waste. When everyone agrees on a certain number of zeroes — zero inventories, zero delays, zero defects, zero breakdowns — providing display boards in work areas becomes essential. Thus, a direct correlation between diversity of indicators in work areas and a firm's level of manufacturing sophistication is not coincidental. Diversity of indicators — independent of their level of performance — is the first point to be considered in diagnosing manufacturing methods.

DECENTRALIZED INDICATORS

The chart in Figure 6-1 records oil deliveries at the Citroën plant in Caen. When the engineering unit adopted the goal of reducing the amount of oil that machines use, it did not seek information only from centralized analytical accounting records; it placed a chart beside every machine.

This is an example of a decentralized indicator. Measurements are performed at locations where oil is used. The indicator is directly visible, and results are analyzed by the users themselves. Advantages include: precise information, immediate updating, and simplification of administrative functions. Moreover, visibility of results encourages everyone's participation in offering ideas about improvements.

The ease with which information can be transmitted has led us astray. To enter anything in a computer is so easy that we overlook the advantages of localized data processing. With a new approach to the use of indicators, however, data processing should be decentralized. Several arguments support this claim.

First, the volume of data argues for decentralization. A vast number of new process indicators has arisen because it is necessary to consider all types of causes and not merely effects. We must observe these factors constantly and interpret them on a

Oil Consumption												
Machines	J	F	M	A	M	J	J	A	S	O	N	D
Broach	60/180	20/160	20/160									
Press 1	20/20	20/20	20/40									
Press 2	40/40	20/100	40/100									
Grinder	20/40	20/60	20/40									
Notching Machine	20/80	20/80	20/60									
Multi-tool	40/40	40/40	20/20									
Total	440	460	420									
Target	500	500	500	400	400	400	400	200	350	350	320	320

oil delivery → | 20/60 | ← cumulative deliveries

Figure 6-1. A chart used at the Citroën plant in Caen to measure oil consumption by individual machines. (The chart measures approximately 3 feet by 6 feet.) The driver who delivers oil is responsible for recording the amounts delivered and computing monthly totals. The chart also records the specified target for the year. Everyone can see the figures and them discussed regularly basis in team meetings. Result: oil consumption for this group of machines has dropped from 8,000 to 4,000 liters in one year.

regular basis. Even a doubling of administrative personnel would be inadequate. Hence, everyone must participate in performing measurements and analysis within his or her own area.

Second, the nature of the problem supports the argument. When the goal is progress, the act of conveying information causes much of its potential to be lost, mainly from the time lag. For phenomena to be interpreted correctly, analyses must be completed quickly.

Furthermore, transmission of information requires information to be detached from its context. This abstraction is not a problem for performance indicators whose role is to facilitate external control. When it is necessary to monitor phenomena in-depth by relying on process indicators, however, detachment of the information becomes a monumental barrier.

Process indicators are usually intended for use by people who work in the particular processes. These are the indicators a coach discusses with players after a game to develop conclusions about the team's defensive or offensive strength, its mobility, its ability to control the ball, and its ability to execute careful maneuvers.

Few of these factors are useful to the team's treasurer, who is mainly concerned with revenues from seats in the stadium. Even if the treasurer skillfully analyzes receipts, he will never discover the indicators that allow anyone to determine what the team must do to play better.

Results indicators are primarily intended for *control*, whereas process indicators are intended to allow *self-control and self-improvement*. The range of process indicators displayed (and kept up-to-date) in a plant is a sign of the employees' integration of their production resources.

THE CULTURAL DIMENSION

When I lecture on visual organization of factories, I use slides from the facilities I have visited for my research. Observing the audience's reactions, I witness an unusual phenomenon. When a large chart indicating absences, which is displayed in some work areas, appears on the screen, I see a sudden increase in curiosity in the audience. (Figure 6-2)

They obviously think: "Aha! Here's something interesting. At last, here's a way of reducing absenteeism in my plant! Now the slackers will practically announce who they are!" A plant owner who would be tempted to apply a *glasnost* policy by displaying this kind of chart at the entrance to the plant would risk serious discomfiture among workers. A certain level of prudence is required in this domain. Attitudes about the types of information that can be disclosed within a company milieu are not the same from Japan to France to the United States.

In most instances, the use of indicators that draw attention to individuals requires caution. The Japanese are very open in

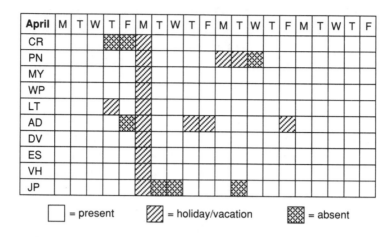

Figure 6-2. Attendance monitoring chart.

this respect, but their boundaries between the individual and the group differ from ours. Are westerners prepared to adopt the same procedures as the Fuji Valve Company?[2] At its automobile valve plant, a small chart intended for self-evaluation is situated beside each work station. (Figure 6-3) The chart is completed on the basis of the workers' agreement with the supervisor, and it is visible to everyone who passes by.

The Importance of the Mode of Presentation

One cannot display indicators without considering the company's internal culture. A small firm will make different choices than a large firm; a recently built plant will have greater freedom than a plant influenced by a long tradition of authoritarian control.

A firm's internal culture can evolve, however. Fortunately, management can learn openness. In addition, ways of presenting information profoundly influence interpretations. When a docu-

---

[2] Excerpt from a report concerning a study mission. Université Louis Pasteur, Strasbourg, France.

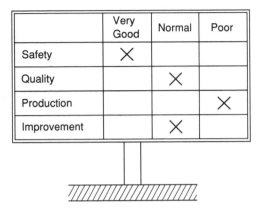

	Very Good	Normal	Poor
Safety	X		
Quality		X	
Production			X
Improvement		X	

Figure 6-3. The Fuji Valve Company, Japan. Chart for individual self-evaluation.

ment is displayed, two messages are conveyed. One is the information itself. The other is the way in which information is presented, and especially the context for which it is intended.

To a varying degree, the influence of the context is observable for all of the indicators we are examining. Let us analyze methods of presenting two critical indicators: absenteeism and diversity of skills.[3]

Absenteeism as an Indicator

At the Renault plant in Sandouville, to monitor for absenteeism each team possesses its own chart, which is included on the principal board for indicators. (Figure 6-4; an overall view is provided in Figure 6-16). Two observations arise:

- First, absences are recorded on the board used to schedule vacation time. Thus, absenteeism is seen as one component

---

[3] At times, it has been thought necessary to banish the term *absenteeism* and instead speak of "presenteeism." However, if one alters a term on a monitoring document – without the team's truly gaining more responsibility for managing its manpower – no meaningful change in the way of perceiving the phenomenon occurs.

of anticipatory tracking of the staffing level. Before discussing the goal of reducing absences, emphasize the need to anticipate them. For a team to function effectively, it needs to plan its resources.

- Second, the board does not list the *names* of absent workers but the total *number* of absentees. The intent is clear. The team's way of managing its work force is the only concept publicly communicated.

Obviously this situation does not eliminate ledgers to maintain records pertaining to individual team members. Information about individuals remains in the private domain and is governed by a restricted relationship between team leaders and members. Private information is available in greater detail than on the chart. A team leader maintains close contact with the members, and is the person most capable of evaluating each member's behavior.

The chart in Figure 6-2 clearly demonstrates the difference. In one instance, absenteeism *per se* is indicated, and displaying

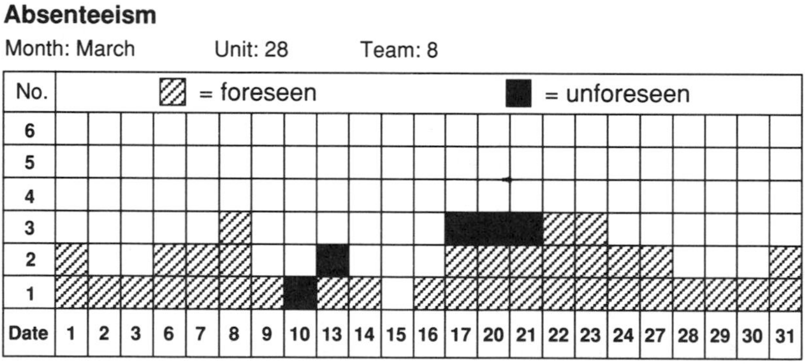

Absenteeism

Month: March   Unit: 28   Team: 8

No.	▨ = foreseen								■ = unforeseen														
6																							
5																							
4																							
3						▨								■	■	▨							
2	▨			▨	▨		■				▨	▨	▨	▨	▨	▨	▨						▨
1	▨	▨	▨	▨	▨	■	▨	▨		▨	▨	▨	▨	▨	▨	▨	▨	▨	▨	▨	▨	▨	▨
Date	1	2	3	6	7	8	9	10	13	14	15	16	17	20	21	22	23	24	27	28	29	30	31

Figure 6-4. A staffing management chart at the Renault plant, Sandouville. The numbers on the left do not represent specific individuals, but rather the total number of people absent. Colors indicate differences between scheduled and actual absences.

this information imparts a moral connotation. In the other instance, a control element is displayed; absenteeism is merely one component. Thus, reframing the information within a broader context can facilitate the displaying of this indicator.

Communicating Diversity of Skill

Many firms are developing more flexible modes of organization for responding effectively to the needs of different markets. Versatility is in demand. For example, a chart displayed at the Citroën plant indicates diversity of skills. (Figure 6-5)

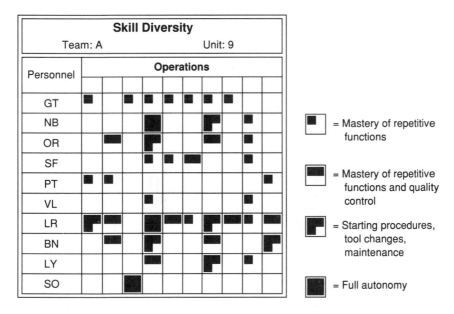

Figure 6-5. The Citroën plant. This form is displayed in production units to chart skill development. The squares are filled as different functions are learned. This chart expresses two components of versatility: ability to operate different work stations (under the heading "Operations") and ability to perform multiple functions at one work station (an area inside the square is filled in).

Apart from easy readability, a grid format offers ease of communication. The firm could have displayed a list of employees, indicating each individual's skills. The list would have been a conventional control document, based on individuals. A grid format, however, expresses versatility as a component of attributes of the work team. Grids allow two forms of interpretation. Horizontally, they indicate an individual's versatility; vertically, they indicate the feasibility of finding someone able to cover an operation at a work station. Hence, when the vertical line is examined, one can assess objective attributes of the production unit. By examining the horizontal line, one identifies how individual workers contribute to this characteristic.

Because of the mode of presentation — a chart — this indicator gains a new connotation. The chart that indicates employees' versatility constitutes a flexibility chart for the production unit. Versatility is nothing more than a way to attain flexibility. In other applications, the chart is a way to improve customer service.[4]

Summary

Displaying indicators does not merely consist of placing management's control charts in the workplace. Rather, the very way of conceiving the system of measurement must change:

- Process indicators are more strongly emphasized.
- Acquisition, measurement, presentation, and analysis of data are decentralized.
- Placing results in the public domain requires consideration of the cultural aspects of the specific type of measurement.

---

[4] The relationship between indicators and their context is always important. (Figure 6-23)

The remainder of this chapter will discuss some practical aspects of using indicators. The conditions required for success will be covered for the stages of selecting indicators, creating boards, starting the project, and ensuring continuity.

SELECTING INDICATORS

Selection of indicators depends on companies' manufacturing policies, ways of organizing plants, and production processes. A facility that produces equipment for the automobile industry does not need the same indicators as a plant that produces customized printed circuits. A plant pursuing a just-in-time project does not use the same indicators as a plant without this kind of activity.

Hence, it is difficult to be general. The following list includes indicators that have been displayed in certain plants. Scrutiny of this list generates several observations.

First, numerous process indicators are included, although this aspect is not surprising. A typical example of an indicator that reflects the logistical quality of production processes is the continuity of the production flow. This indicator allows the determination of a suitable weekly distribution of the monthly production volume. Distribution is not always highly consistent. Delays arise at the beginning of the month — from shortages of materials, out-of-service machines and so on — and at the end of the month, when, to meet quotas, efforts are undertaken to complete products that are only semi-completed.

Moreover, many of these indicators have no equivalent in the accounting systems. Examples include percentages of orders delivered on time, levels of accuracy in measuring inventory, or length of time without breakdowns. This lack of parallelism can be explained by the change in the role of measurements. In a conventional context, each indicator must be oriented toward the balance sheet and the profit-and-loss statement. Phenomena that do not produce directly measurable bookkeeping results are overlooked.

Thus, the policies of some firms approach the absurd, as they stubbornly track pennies while failing to measure availability of inventories, flow duration, or indicators of the reliability of machinery.[5]

We have also noted the presence of several indicators intended to track dispersions, distributions, or profiles, a trend reflecting companies' efforts to stabilize the production process.

An overall approach to production, cited in regard to visual control, underlies this objective: A plant refrains from increasing volumes or speeds until the principal parameters have been successfully understood and controlled. Managers have less interest in trains' maximum speeds and more interest in trains' ability to arrive on time, and the factors that enable them to do so.

Last, several indicators have been created for monitoring projects, solving problems, or determining whether policies are being implemented suitably.

1. Flows
   - Average production lead time and variance
   - Productivity
   - Fulfillment of commitments (deadlines, quantities)
   - Volume of semi-finished items
   - Flow profile: continuity, regularity, throughput time
2. Materials and inventories
   - Monitoring of unavailable items in warehouses (materials or finished products)

---

[5] Affirming that indicators are not *accounting indicators* does not mean exiling dollars and cents from the workplace. Financial conversions are always useful. For example, one can multiply reclaimed space by the cost per square foot or multiply downtime by the per-hour cost of a given machine. The intent, however, is improving communication, instead of ensuring that results fit into an accounting framework.

- Quantity of material needed to build one unit of good product
- Inventory volume and turnover
- Warehouse management performance (response time, accuracy of inventories)

3. Technical resources
   - Availability of machinery
   - Yield level (output quantity divided by input quantity)
   - Breakdown rates, or production time without problems
   - Time needed for changing production runs
   - Maintenance costs in relation to production units
   - Percentages of preventive/remedial maintenance
   - Number and duration of technical assistance calls
   - Average length of repair periods

4. Quality
   - Percentages of unacceptable items
   - Rejection and retouching rates
   - Results of quality audits
   - Total cost of not meeting quality standards
   - Period of operation without major problems.

5. Clients and suppliers
   - Sales volume
   - Delivery time
   - Customer-satisfaction indicators: quality, service, number of problems.

6. Employees
   - Labor supply
   - Number of suggestions (proposed, implemented)
   - Hours of training
   - Level of skill diversity within the teams
   - Absenteeism

7. Work Environment
   - Housekeeping indicator
   - Safety audits
   - Work accidents

8. Overhead
   • Monitoring of team's costs
   • Power, oil, small tools, etc.
9. Miscellaneous
   • Number of products covered by quality assurance
   • Number of automatic devices installed on equipment
   • Number of quality circles
   • Number of machines monitored with statistical process control (SPC)
   • Distribution of occupied space
   • Level of standardization of components

DEFINING MEASUREMENTS AND UNITS

The act of displaying an indicator does not fundamentally modify the way measurement is performed. Nevertheless, pay close attention to two aspects:

   • Interpretation of results must be easy for everyone.
   • Simplify computations. Measuring phenomena with exceptional precision in every instance is not necessary. To select a measurement that provides an approximate result is often as effective for interpretation as using a specific measurement.

For example, a plant that produces machinery has adopted the goal of monitoring the time required for changing the type of production. The first idea is to graph the times on a chart. During the research phase, however, two observations emerge. One is that making a precise measurement itself requires time. After consideration, the group pursuing this project concludes that measurement does not require a precision of seconds. At the start a reading precise to a ten-minute range is sufficient.
   Second, the purpose of the graph is not to trace the precise chronology of the phenomenon but to know generally what the

average tendency is, how this tendency stands in relation to the objective, and the dispersion during a given month.

The chart in Figure 6-6 is designed according to these criteria. With each change in production, the timekeeper determines elapsed time and places a circular sticker in one of the areas divided into ten-minute intervals. At the end of the month, without processing any data, a clear histogram emerges indicating the distribution of results in relation to the objective as well as trends from one month to the next. By measuring the dispersion, one can determine whether certain changes in tooling were especially rapid, and others particularly slow, and then develop relevant conclusions.

Selecting Units of Measurement

Whereas the selection of units of measurement is not extremely important for performing computations, when the goal is communication, the situation is entirely different. To announce a defect rate of 4,000 parts per million (ppm) conveys that a significant margin for improvement exists, whereas calling

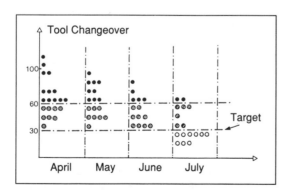

Figure 6-6. Chart for recording tool changeover time for changing production series. The vertical scale is divided into three zones. The supervisor uses a sticker with a different color in each zone.

it 0.4% makes doing better appear inconceivable. Saying that twelve minutes are needed for changing a tool is more effective than calling it one-fifth of an hour.

Some forms of measurement are preferable because they are less abstract, though they may be less specific in mathematical terms. For example, "238 accident-free days in the machining unit" creates a much stronger impression than "an accident rate of .0002." Indicating that a machine operated for 32 hours without the slightest malfunction is not a practical form of measurement for consolidating data for the entire plant, but for people who have seen the machine operate without stopping

Date: _____	**Neatness Survey**				Visitors: _____	
Department	Cigarette Butts	Papers	Cans/ Bottles	Plastic Items	Metal Scraps	Other*
Stamping						
Parts						
Bodies						
Painting						
Assembly						
Plating						
Machining						
Stairways and Bathrooms:	No. _____	No. _____	No. _____	No. _____	No. _____	No. _____

*Specify: _____

Stairway numbers are indicated on each door.
Place an "X" in the appropriate box.

Figure 6-7. The Renault plant, Sandouville. This document for assessing the level of housekeeping is completed by visitors, who indicate their opinions about neatness and orderliness in the plant. The results are displayed in the plant's main corridor.

for four entire days, the period of time expresses an extremely precise concept.

Qualitative Measurements

Development of process indicators has led to the inclusion of numerous qualitative parameters on the scoreboards of individual teams or production units. For example, include indicators for neatness and orderliness. The simplest method is a brief questionnaire that indicates fundamental characteristics that must be monitored. (Figure 6-7)

Figure 6-8. The Renault plant. In the plant's main corridor, this board indicates the results of visitors' evaluations of neatness and orderliness. Each month, three departments are awarded a place on the winner's podium.

The main captions on the left say, "Sandouville: A clean plant — every day, every week, every month." The map below the podium points out the location of the three winners for the month.

DESIGNING CHARTS

Avoid Overloading

In portraying phenomena in which they are involved, people often tend toward excess. Undue enthusiasm, too much data, or too much complexity may play a role.

From the standpoint of those observing charts, simplicity is an advantage. Displaying a chart of minimal data allows the team to save time in updating and conveys a message that will be more clearly understood.

Organize information on two levels: one for rapid overall perception, sufficient for understanding major trends, and the second for more detail. A large curve or other symbol can indicate a general tendency. The document should be mounted or suspended to be clearly visible to everyone.

The second level of communication presents additional information, either in small print on the same document, or on

Figure 6-9. Large chart (approximately 3 feet high) hanging from the ceiling, at the J. Reydel plant in Gondecourt. It conveys simple information to the entire unit regarding productivity, quality, materials consumption, defects, most recent accident, and absenteeism. More detailed indicators appear on other charts.

another document on a rack, to provide clarification, or for discussions in a meeting area.

Make It Large and Colorful

Since information must be visible at a distance, large-scale charts, usually to be filled in by hand, are preferable to dense graphs generated by computers. Rely on colors, and, as often as possible, use graphs to attract attention and facilitate immediate overall comprehension.

Express goals clearly at all times. The same observation is true for goals and reality. (Ways to set goals will be discussed further in this chapter.) Using different colors can immediately show whether or not targets are being met.

Because production teams complete graphs themselves, the workers should not require six months of art school to update the graphs. Using adhesive dots and strips or magnetic · markers is a simple way to obtain professional-looking results. Even if a curve is drawn hesitantly, the overall appearance can still be attractive.

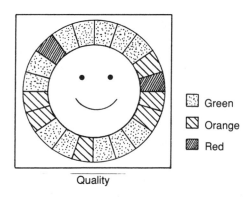

Quality

Figure 6-10. A chart at the NUMMI plant in Fremont, California, indicating combined results (quality, absenteeism, deadlines). Each segment represents one day. The expression on the face in the middle emphasizes the quality of overall results.

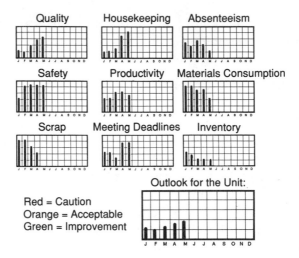

Figure 6-11. A series of monthly indicators (approximately 3 feet by 5 feet) on the wall in a unit at the J. Reydel plant in Gondecourt. Each column could appear in one of three colors, depending on the trend. Red means caution, decrease, a critical threshold. Orange means acceptable, but improvement is possible. Green means a situation corresponding to fixed objectives, or improvements. The overall outlook for the unit is determined by obtaining the average for the nine indicators.

Standardizing Rules of Illustration

To someone who wants to see certain results at a glance, spending ten minutes learning about the semi-logarithmic scale or the three-dimensional abacus is a waste of time. Furthermore, if yellow is a sign of success in the machining section, but represents a disaster in the assembly section, communication is hampered. Adopt shared principles for certain vital aspects: selection of units, modes of portrayal, color, signs, and symbols. Thus, a red sticker can mean that a goal has not been met; a green one can indicate that it has been surpassed.

Some firms attempt to ensure that the slope of a curve always possesses the same meaning: rising, conditions are favorable; descending, they are unfavorable. This interesting concept often leads to practical problems in selecting forms of

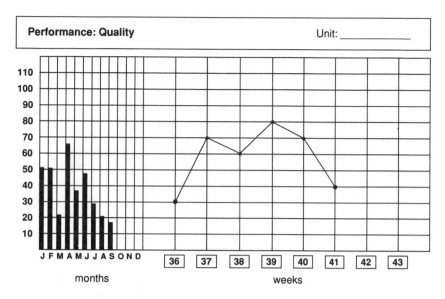

Figure 6-12. A chart in the pressing section at the Renault plant, Sandouville. The machinists keep the chart up to date, simultaneously presenting annual and weekly performance. The curves are produced with removable tape, so that the weekly chart can be begun again at the end of each quarter. Figure 6-20 depicts the board on which this chart is mounted.

measurement. Increasing the percentage of acceptable components from 98.4% to 99.2% is less impressive than reducing the percentage of defective components from 1.6% to 0.8%. Often, it is simpler to provide an arrow to indicate the direction of progress, or to add symbols of acknowledgment when a given measurement shows improvement.

Standardization, Not Uniformity

Standardizing modes of illustration does not mean that every board should be designed the same way from one unit to the next. Selection and organization of indicators depend significantly upon the structure of production units. In addition, it is better for each team to contribute a personal touch to its own charts.

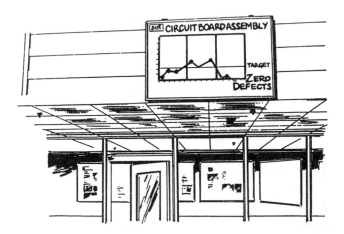

Figure 6-13. Large charts (approximately 3 feet by 6 feet) placed at entrances to the main units in the Bull plant in Angers. Most of these charts show measurements of quality indicators (in a total quality sense, including quality of logistical processes, such as meeting of deadlines).

Personalization should not hinder comprehension. Instead, personalization strongly affects esthetic elements, such as decoration, accessories, or frames.

An appropriate strategy is to encourage a team to pursue initiatives in structuring its own communication space. Allow the placement of other information around a chart, such as news about markets, information concerning new products or a recently installed machine. The setting enriches the chart, allowing it to become more attractive and fully integrated with the team's activities.

The working group that is responsible for the project should distinguish between elements requiring standardization, for which precise requirements must be defined, and elements that can be left to the initiative of each group.

Symbolic Representation

A motorist's right foot suddenly lightens on the gas pedal as he drives past an accident where rescue workers are extricating the victims. Seeing statistics arranged in rows is one thing, but seeing a body lying on a stretcher is another.

Whenever possible, rely on concrete means of displaying information. Such means should be closely associated with the phenomenon being portrayed. Everyone feels more deeply affected by concrete phenomena than by abstract representations.

In some cases one can use indicators that are associated with the objects themselves. Examples include displaying a floor space newly freed up by improvements (Figure 7-9), or a visible level of rejected items in a red container. Nevertheless, this form of representation has practical limitations.

An alternative solution is to display information oriented toward the right side of the brain, which is sensible to colors and visual portrayal. The right side is also the source of emotions.

In addition to offering quickness of perception, symbols reinforce basic information and cause it to live by evoking a certain context. Poclain's sketch of a power shovel (Figure 6-17) is a good example. If quality ratios improve, the shovel operates more effectively, digging a deeper hole.

Media techniques currently used in advertising or audiovisual material frequently rely on these forms of portrayal. For

Figure 6-14. The Kawasaki Motors plant in Akashi, Japan. The time elapsed when the assembly line is shut down is indicated cumulatively on a clock hanging in the center of the work area. (Technically, a board with digital figures is also suitable.) The figure communicated is a concrete indication of time lost by the entire unit. The clock stimulates the same type of awareness in everyone as wearing a watch and reinforces the sense of membership in the group.

example, consider the symbol that conveys the results of legislative elections on French television: A semicircle representing the French National Assembly is shown, with members' seats distributed according to electoral results.

Encourage teams to display originality. Workers' direct involvement in selecting forms of expression or symbols promotes their assimilation of new modes of communication.

SELECTING LOCATIONS

Avoid placing charts randomly when a new need arises, without paying adequate attention to coherence of communication.

Indicators must become tools, in the same way that teams use stamping presses, programmable robots, or tools made of

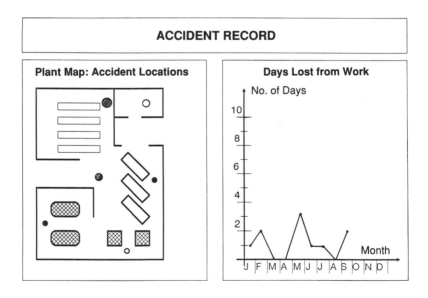

Figure 6-15. A chart for presenting accident statistics. The image of the plant layout, using stickers of different colors and shapes to indicate types and frequency of accidents, enhances the impact of the message.

Figure 6-16. An assembly team at the Renault Sandouville plant decided to portray certain indicators with automotive speed indicators. The needle positions indicate whether the measured characteristic is in the optimal zone or the red zone.

tempered steel. At all costs avoid taping pieces of paper hastily to the walls, because such papers reveal the marginal nature of this attempt to communicate.

Create an authentic communication area where employees meet to discuss results. If possible, provide one area for each team. Otherwise, provide a common area where each group encounters relevant charts.

Highlight this area. Some factories apply a fresh coat of paint to the floor or the wall. Other factories provide a few green plants or a decor that emphasizes a convivial atmosphere. Any decisions about appearance and location should be made with employee participation.

Generally anything that enriches the environment for indicators is beneficial. An appropriate arrangement may consist of placing products manufactured by the work unit around the

Carvin Plant

Digging Away At the Difference !

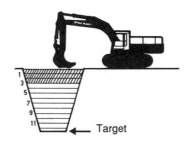

Target

Figure 6-17. Poclain's plant in Carvin, France, decided on the power shovel as a symbol for portraying progress in quality improvement, reduction of semi-finished items, and cost reduction. The shovel deepens the hole at the pace at which production improves.

chart. (Figure 6-19) In some plants, photographs of results obtained by progress groups are placed beside indicators.

In the United States, I often encountered photographs of a production team's history: installation of a new machine, development of a prototype, or a celebration of the achievement of an objective.

A Geometry Problem

Because displays are intended not only for teams' internal discussions but also for contact with the external environment, their locations should, to the greatest possible extent, be along boundaries between a team's territory and passageway. These locations should be both internally and externally visible. (See the arrangement adopted by certain teams at the Citroën plant

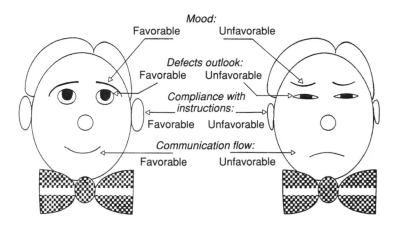

Figure 6-18. The Samsung Electromechanics plant in Korea uses this "Quality Boy," a wooden figure with movable parts. Each team has one of these figures in its work area. Every month, the workers adjust the eyes, ears, mouth, and eyebrows according to joint evaluations completed by the team and management.

Figure 6-19. An auto body at the Renault Sandouville plant. The presence of a product in the shop offers two advantages. The practical advantage is that it allows discussion of defects in a concrete manner. The symbolic advantage is that seeing the product compensates for the abstract nature of graphs.

in Figure 6-21.) If one must choose, it is better to dissociate information. A simplified representation should be visible from outside the work area; more detailed indicators should be inwardly oriented.

Lack of Space

Companies that display their results often encounter a lack of space. The walls quickly reach the saturation point, especially if large-scale charts are selected, as is advisable.

There are multiple complementary solutions. One is to organize information by priority. The most prominent locations should be allocated vital points and summaries, whereas other information can be organized in less prominent locations (using rotary panels, for example).

Panels can be placed on the floor, as in exhibition booths, or hung from the ceiling, or mounted high on the walls. This approach works only for extremely simple, oversized graphs. Some companies use different sides of a cube or a trihedron, placed on a stand or suspended.

Updating can be performed either by lowering the panels, if an appropriate method of securing them has been selected, or by using a lifting device or a ladder.

STARTING PROJECTS

Executives can easily agree about the precise meaning of a performance indicator. By working together, everyone ultimately gains an understanding of what terms mean. An entirely different situation arises, however, with attempts to display indicators. How can we be sure that the indicators strike the same chord in everyone who encounters them?

The problem resembles the previously cited problem of displaying production objectives. For a display to be effective, the same culture must exist in a company.

Can we be sure that the firm's chief financial officer is not the only one who regards inventories as a burden? Have we not encountered production units that secretly adore it when the warehouses are overflowing, because keeping large supplies of materials on hand means that job security is not in danger? Have we not likewise encountered plants where the machine shutdowns that torment the person in charge of scheduling are regarded as a blessing by the mechanics? Under these conditions, what would be the impact of charts indicating the curve for inventory and the curve for reliability of machinery? Preparation is needed, perhaps over several months to disseminate shared ideas about the firm's functioning and objectives.

Providing Training in Advance

Training is one factor that enables the work force to attain the necessary level of understanding before a project begins. Two aspects are involved.

The first is assimilation of management's fundamental ideas of the directions that must be followed in order for the firm to make progress. Marketing strategy, quality, production control, measurement of costs, use of materials and human resources, safety, and continuous improvement are among the necessary concepts that ensure that everyone will know how to situate indicators within a precise perspective.

Training explains the motivations that govern displaying of indicators. This occasion is suitable for indicating that management's purpose is not to pass judgment on people, but to endow them with a new tool for communication and thought.

This tool allows greater precision. (No one says, "They're always behind" any more; instead, an indicator for delays is introduced.) This tool promotes dialogue and offers opportunities to create contacts. A team's indicators are also of interest to the technical, methods, and purchasing divisions, among others.

General knowledge must be supplemented by a second, more technical level of training. Certain confusing terms must be clarified. What is a target? What is a standard? What is a differential? Elementary techniques of measurement, selection of pertinent parameters, selection of units, types of graphs, and drawings of curves are topics that must be covered before the first charts are displayed.

Team Participation in Designing Charts

As a result of training, teams will be able to participate in the project extremely directly: selecting indicators, designing graphs, and producing charts. These activities should not be left entirely to a team. Some indicators are shared by the entire plant, so coordination is necessary. Also, various departments may provide assistance.

In every case, the essential consideration is that a team should not feel dispossessed. The project for displaying indicators is, above all, the team's own project.

A Pilot Location

Introduction of displayed information should occur gradually. The pilot-location method, beginning with a representative section, is usually advantageous:

- The project group may not consider every factor initially. Inevitably, certain changes will be introduced. A pilot location allows improvements to occur.
- Because the initial attempt constitutes a trial, it is easier to obtain participation by team members.
- A pilot team can obtain visible results extremely quickly. Dissemination throughout the plant is then easy. People talk, examine, observe, and reflect. Curiosity accomplishes the rest. A member of the working group that successfully

implemented the first project can be given the responsibility of aiding the rest of the plant to follow the group's example.

The Right Moment

According to Mr. Hue, an assistant to the head of the assembly division at the Renault plant, one must wait for a suitable time to start a display project. "It's necessary to avoid illusions," he says. "Even if there's some curiosity in the beginning, a board isn't always a permanent attraction by itself. Interest is only generated insofar as a chart answers specific questions team members have."

Preparatory efforts should therefore concentrate on questions instead of on responses. When employees ask certain questions, the proper time for starting a project has arrived.

Providing Information

When the Renault plant decides to develop a new board for displaying indicators in the assembly line, it establishes a small working group. This group includes management personnel, technicians, and machinists. The project leader is Mr. Descamps, a manager directing approximately 60 people in teams on the line, but the project is developed to allow subsequent coverage of the entire division.

Mr. Descamps's way of proceeding to ensure promotion of the project is similar to a properly organized marketing campaign:

> I'm in charge of putting up indicators throughout the department. Each unit should display results related to its activities. In a working group, we defined how indicators should be computed and presented. Now I need to promote the idea in my work area. I thought that I should be selling

this idea. I was able to get an estimate from a student enterprise at a university in Le Havre. Two students helped me design booklets and panels like the ones used in advertising.

Creating curiosity means relying on original ideas. When you're walking down a street, there are some ads you don't look at any more. On the other hand, when someone is putting up a new poster, people pay attention. Some people even stop and wait to see what the poster will say.

That's how the idea came to me. For my next campaign, I developed a set of posters that can be put up like flags during the day, without distracting anyone. The results are a sure thing — during the break, the workers will ask, "Exactly what is this indicator project about?" Then I will say, "Look, here's a booklet. You'll find everything explained there."

When the project for displaying indicators in the stamping unit of the Renault plant began, a working group was formed with help from two business students. For an hour every day during a two-month period the group met to define key parameters, select indicators and rules of computation, and define ways to display results and lay out boards. One of the students states:

This was a truly enriching experience. The act of defining performance indicators made it necessary to reach agreement within the group about what seemed important. This was an unparalleled opportunity to look at the workers' perspectives in relation to management's viewpoint.

After several lively meetings, we agreed on the factors to be monitored. Then we worked on how to measure parameters. For example, for maintaining the working environment, we developed an evaluation form to be completed by a member of the production team. This document is a list of key points: oil spots on the floor, inventory or extraneous items in a given area, order in the aisles and machine areas, storage of spare parts in cabinets, neatness of the break area, condition of trash cans, and so on.

This list was designed to be completed quickly. It takes only five minutes every morning to complete this mini-evaluation. The team records the average for the entire week on the board. (Figure 6-20)

In terms of the computation method, our training made us emphasize accuracy and detail. This emphasis is a mistake, however. It's better to use an approximate indicator that's directly related to the phenomenon being observed, instead of an overly sophisticated indicator that employees could not easily associate with concrete phenomena.

Figure 6-20. Board of indicators for the pressing unit at the Renault Sandouville plant. The indicators are: maintenance of the work environment (housekeeping, safety); quality; reliability of machines (measured by ability to respond to kanban tickets); time required for tool changeover and for attaining a standard rate of production.

After testing the charts for two months, we arrived at the phase where objectives must be defined. During the first meeting, management asked employees to commit themselves for three months to major objectives in four areas: maintenance of the work environment, availability of machinery, changing of production series, and quality. The three-month objectives were not defined by management. Its role was to highlight the department's orientations and priorities.

In a subsequent meeting, the supervisors and technical specialists indicated the available resources for attaining these objectives. After an hour of negotiation, an agreement was established. When the project was developed, the group's work was presented to a hundred people in a forum, a meeting where improvement teams present results.[6]

The boards evoked considerable curiosity in teams from other work areas when they met with their coworkers in the stamping unit. The working group wanted the charts to be esthetically appealing. A production representative suggested that the floor be repainted where boards were being set up. Now these areas are neat and attractive.

The other day, some Germans visited the plant. They spent at least fifteen minutes in front of the boards, which indicates their level of interest. You can imagine how proud the entire unit was!

DEFINING OBJECTIVES

Displaying results without providing ways for employees to initiate action on behalf of progress is like offering a scale to an obese person without providing any information about proper nutrition. The scale cannot promote weight loss. Indeed, it may only produce discouragement. Factories are similar. A person will not be interested in the indicator curves unless he or she is

---

6 See Chapter 7, page 234.

convinced that the results are not merely coincidental. People must be convinced that they can influence the curves if they set their minds to it.

Indicators should never be displayed without allowing opportunities for the workers to improve the phenomenon the charts represented. The objective on a board constitutes a line of sight for the entire team, and for everyone capable of contributing to success.

The requirements for selecting objectives are comparable to those cited for production objectives in Chapter 4:

- Objectives should be realistic. They should be accessible by the means being adopted and steps being taken on behalf of progress.
- The purpose is not to surpass goals, but to attain them. To maintain a specific result successfully (because doing so demonstrates that the situation is under control) is more important than to achieve feats that lead nowhere.
- Objectives should be set as the result of consensus, so that everyone who is involved is mobilized in the same direction.

At the Télémécanique plant, teams' yearly plans are prepared in the same way for the entire firm, from the machinists to the managers. Once a year, the division's managers prepare their own plan, and present it to all of the employees in a general meeting. Then a succession of plans is developed in descending order, with each executive transmitting between the team to which he or she belongs and the team that he or she heads.

The production-team leader prepares a plan with a group of volunteers. At least ten hours, divided into several meetings, are usually needed to obtain a satisfactory outcome. Then the small group presents the plan to the rest of the team.

The plan consists of three phases: diagnosis, objectives, and the plan for action. Management gives the team an official guide to develop the outcome for each of these three phases. The same document is used by the management team and by basic teams in production units.

Defining objectives takes several rules into account: objectives should be measurable, limited in number, and attainable. Moreover, consensus is reached in the process of discussion.

As one manager indicates, the establishment of objectives is a delicate process: "A certain finesse is required. We have to seek enough consistency with the objectives of the highest level in the hierarchy, without imposing objectives that the team would see itself as unable to attain.

"Choices need to be shaped," she added, "without being forced upon the participants. We have observed that, so long as this procedure has existed, it has had extremely favorable effects upon employees' ability to plan results. People are aware of their capabilities, so when we establish an objective, in most instances, it will be accomplished."

This preparatory process may seem cumbersome, compared with posting a chart on a wall and defining objectives by drawing red lines for the next month. To omit this phase, however, risks the objectives becoming a mirage rather than a commitment.

At the Télémécanique plant, commitment has emerged as a distinctive component of the firm's culture. In an interview with members of a production team, I asked them about the motive that inspired them to pursue the indicated objectives. Their reply was instinctive: "Our honor is on the line."

CONTINUOUS UPDATING

When Mr. Savoye, the manager of Renault's Sandouville plant, sees an indicator document that has not been updated for several weeks, he arranges to remove it from the work area: "If a document has not been completed," he explains, "it means that people are not convinced of its usefulness. If we let it remain as is, we are showing that displaying of indicators is imposed by the top level. This is absolutely the opposite of our approach."

Maintaining charts when most users have ceased to be interested in them is a trap many firms cannot easily avoid. When the charts are first mounted, they benefit from a high level of curiosity. Everyone looks at them to see whether the curves are rising or declining, and to wonder whether tomorrow's sky will be cloudy or sunny. It is difficult to sustain this kind of interest during subsequent months.

A Voluntary Approach to Updating

If the management outlook that governs displaying of indicators includes furnishing useful information, distributing a statement that has been previously prepared without team input is an error. Intending to proceed correctly, some people believe they can save time because the document is ready to be displayed, but the only means of ensuring that the indicator will continue to generate interest is lost along the way. The graph will always be kept up to date, but no one will know whether the employees truly need it.

The team should therefore do the updating. Team members should not necessarily perform every calculation and prepare every document. A voluntary link must exist, however, within the processing chain. Even if statistics or graphs are generated by a computer, employees should participate actively in displaying the results, by continuing to transfer data manually from a computer screen onto a large chart, for example. Thus weakening of the link is readily visible.

This is truly visual communication. Instead of thrusting information upon potential users, one allows them to express a need. Information is requested from downstream, in keeping with the self- service principle.[7]

Insufficient Time

Some plant managers fear that information updating may cause employees in production units to lose significant amounts of time. While there are many new indicators, these indicators are widely dispersed and decentralized. Each small team is responsible for monitoring three or four of them. Thus, updating requires only a few minutes a day.

At the same time, concepts of how production workers' time should be spent are evolving. Time in a factory is no longer wholly allocated to producing parts. (Furthermore, the belief that employees truly spend their time only in production is an illusion for some managers, especially considering unexpected interruptions.)

Employees have begun to assume responsibility for new functions. This change is especially noticeable in plants that are adopting a just-in-time approach. When an item manufactured at upstream locations is no longer needed at downstream locations, it is imperative to halt production of the item. Because it is not always possible to manufacture some other product, employees should be capable of performing tasks on a staggered schedule. Updating indicators, assuming responsibility for visual documentation, and analyzing results are useful work that does not generate inventory.

---

[7] Microcomputers are very convenient for this type of work. Nevertheless, ensure from the outset that an orientation consistent with of this type of hardware — a decentralized tool — is adopted. At Physio-Control, documents for production units are not prepared on microcomputers until the unit is capable of preparing the document itself.

MAINTAINING A DIALOGUE

"When I want to discuss results with the members of a team," a unit manager for Ernault Toyota told me, "I say, 'So, how did it go today? Let's look at the chart!'"

"Then we go to the large panel where indicators are displayed. I remain silent, and I don't make any comments. If the charts are properly done, I shouldn't be the first person to say something. I can wait for the person next to me to provide a spontaneous interpretation of the results. She's the one who explains what happened during the past week. If there were problems, she tells me why. If things went well, I also ask why. I avoid letting the conversation focus upon problems all the time. It's also necessary to talk about what goes well."

Management by Wandering Around

The term for this style of management by direct contact is "Management By Wandering Around" (MBWA). MBWA is not taking a stroll, shaking hands, bestowing smiles, and saying "Hi, how's it going with your house remodeling, the fishing contest, your child's birthday?" This small talk is not harmful, but is merely politeness.

By decentralizing and providing management tools at the production location, management has in effect expanded the number of managers. Meeting in front of a graph with a team leader and asking what his or her group intends to do to reduce the stamping machine's level of rejects from three percent to two percent is a management conversation. Talking about the status of a project for rapid retooling with machinists, whose schedule appears on the current projects chart, is a management conversation. Asking unit supervisors about problems concerning deadlines with suppliers of boxes is also a management conversation.

Visual communication is a formidable means of stimulating informal contact within a company, promoting direct communication between equals, without a chain of command. The situation no longer involves machinists submitting reports to their supervisors. Instead, two responsible parties exchange observations about reality. The success of a project for displaying information significantly depends upon management's ability to use charts to encourage an ongoing flow of observations, comments, and constructive ideas.

An Invitation to Discussion

The need to create extremely clear charts visible from a distance has been emphasized earlier. How much distance is recommended? Two feet? Twenty feet? There may be no simple answer. One unit manager at the Renault plant in Sandouville envisions the situation in his own domain:

> When you're in your own section you know that anyone going down the aisle — visitors, coworkers, or managers — can tell whether the curve is rising or falling. When seen from a certain distance, however, this information is not enough. Why does the curve go up? Why does it drop?
> When people who pass by raise such questions, they're undoubtedly interested in coming closer, because the rising curve intrigues them. If they're interested, there's a good chance that they'll want to ask questions of anyone who is near the curve. "What's happening in terms of the plan for reducing defects? How did you manage to improve the quality of goods being supplied? Is absenteeism being reduced?" It's important to know that managers passing by may start talking to you. This is a terrific stimulus for having clear opinions about every topic, and for constantly monitoring your results.

This answers my question about the distance at which charts should be legible. A portion of the message should be visible at a suitable distance for anyone who passes by. At the same time, however, being able to distinguish everything is not desirable. The purpose of using displays is not merely to impart information, as in the era of external control, but also to stimulate dialogue.

Passersby should therefore be able to see something that inspires them to come closer — a curve, a color, or a cloud. This is an innovative feature of displays: the insufficiency of the information from a distance gives communication a distinctive dynamic.

Visual communication therefore is a continual invitation to dialogue. This discussion arises if a person passing by engages in a conversation, but it is also an imaginary dialogue between the person working in the territory and a person who passes by without saying anything. The worker knows that the passerby sees the indicator and can guess what the passerby thinks.

A New Role for Shop-level Supervision

If this discussion about displayed documents continues, the role of supervisors in production units will change. People in this role have received little training for the required type of communication, seeking results through influence. When one person instructs another to complete a task, change work stations, or move a dolly, these are orders and the other person's role is to obey.

Today, the challenge is how to persuade, how to motivate groups and people, and how to awaken curiosity. Displaying indicators cannot be successful unless supervisory personnel are prepared for a new mode of communication.

The Daily Scoop

A supervisor at the Citroën plant said that, in seeking to transform the charts into a pole of attraction, he had rediscovered the virtues of advertising.

Because I often shop in supermarkets, I saw that they use a different advertising theme every day. There's always something new to attract customers' attention. I thought I'd do something similar. I put an erasable board beside the graphs, and I write a different message there every day. These are very brief messages about the team's activities or about the firm. "A British client will be visiting us." "A meeting will take place on Monday at 8:00 for clarifying our approach to quality." "The protective gloves have arrived."

This way, the workers come to take a look every day, because they're curious, or because it's sort of like looking at the news on television. When they're there, they take a glance at the curves. I arranged to set up the charts in the aisle, on the other side of my office. Therefore, when one of them stops to look at the curves when I'm in my office, I can go out and say, "What do you think?" Then he'll express his opinion, and a dialogue begins.

ENSURING INTEGRATION OF TEAM PROJECTS

In certain plants, one can observe charts with data or graphs in the main corridors. (Figure 6-22) These are the plant's principal performance indicators, compiling general data. I have saved discussion of these for last because attempting to interest employees in displays of comprehensive information is useless if localized displaying of information has not become habitual.

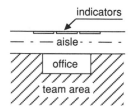

Figure 6-21. The Citroën plant in Caen. Positioning of indicators.

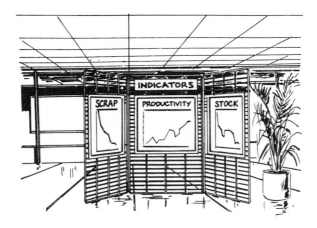

Figure 6-22. Visual indicators at the entrance of the Renault Sandouville plant.

Once employees learn how indicators for their sections function, they will become interested in the indicators in other parts of the plant. Proceed from the specific to the general, and not vice versa.

Achieving harmony between teams' objectives and the company's objectives is not always easy. As with the case of Telemecanique, the process depends significantly on the method adopted when objectives are defined.

The quality of this integration of objectives depends significantly on leadership personnel's efforts. During meetings for production units, team leaders must simultaneously present the team's results and those of the company, to emphasize the connection between the firm's strategies and the way that events unfold in the workplace. (See Figure 6-23)

Every opportunity for reinforcing a sense of unity and coherence should be used. The company newsletter could include a section on production units' results. Use the same indicators for production teams and the entire plant. At Renault, a quality index computed according to the same criteria is simultaneously displayed at the entrance to the plant, in

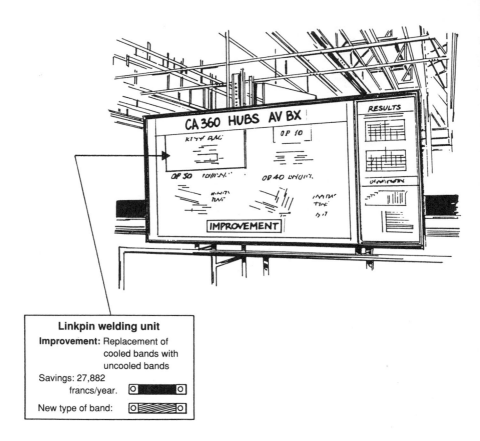

Figure 6-23. The Citroën plant, Caen. Presenting curves for results and a sample of accomplishments that have led to progress is an effective way to reinforce assimilation of indicators an overall context. Someone responsible for a machine where an improvement has taken place can visualize technical advances and their favorable impact on operating results at the same time.

production units, and on teams' boards. Company-wide logos used on charts and badges contribute to a sense of unity. (Figure 6-24)

When the plant has successfully completed efforts to achieve alignment, every employee feels a part of a whole. Mr.

Malherbe, an assistant department manager at the Renault plant, states, "Because of their knowledge of objectives and results, and their understanding of the overall environment, our employees are profoundly aware of their contributions to the firm's competitive capabilities. Everyone has a feeling of contributing a stone to erect a cathedral."

Figure 6-24. The Solex plant, Evreux. When a company project is started, define symbols or slogans to appear on every indicator chart, from the charts displayed in work areas to those visible in managers' offices. A coherence of form strengthens the feel- ing of participating in a collective endeavor. This knight logo is used to symbolize total quality. It appears on the indicator charts and on badges presented to people who have completed certain levels of training.

7

Making Progress
Visible

A few years ago, a suggestion box was installed in a large plant that manufactures electronic components. During the first few months, some suggestions were submitted. Then interest rapidly abated. After a while no one opened the box. A year later, the key had vanished. "At that point," the production manager said, "nobody dared to break the lock, afraid they might find suggestions more than six months old inside."

This is a lamentable fate for an object designed to foster ingenuity, a symbol of human intelligence. The suggestion box not only failed to yield results, but it became a trap, swallowing ideas without returning them.

Why do suggestion boxes in factories yield so few results? There are various reasons. The concept does not rely on a broad enough foundation. Because ideas often arise from the same individuals, a suggestion box can be elitist. Difficult to manage, it lacks its own dynamic and does not generate enthusiasm. Essentially, a suggestion box is an inadequate method for comments that most firms are abandoning.

The company that never opened its suggestion box is an extreme example. This story is true, however, and reveals the inadequacy of traditional ways of promoting participation. If the concept of improvement in factories had not changed during the past decade, however, there would be few reasons to write this chapter. Is there a less visual method than a suggestion box?

Two Components of Improvement

Most firms now recognize that improvement in manufacturing depends on two components. The first component, which is technological, involves altering the structure of the mode of production. New machinery is installed, robots are developed, and more productive technology is created. This process originates outside the workplace.

The second, in the workplace, involves improving efficiency without changing the structure of production. Internal improvement relies directly on observation of reality. Why was this second type of progress ignored for so long?

First, it is difficult for centralized organizations to coordinate a mode of progress that depends on observation of details and leads to numerous small improvements. Second, we are at the end of a growth era, a period of expansion when plants were oriented primarily to developing new resources instead of improving existing resources.

Strategic breakthroughs can easily eclipse other forms of action when vast territory must be conquered, when the terrain permits the deployment of heavy vehicles, and when strength prevails over agility. On the other hand, when it is necessary to maneuver on a limited field, to gain ground slowly, and to master complexity, the ability to analyze and to observe reality reemerges as vital.

This chapter focuses on such analytic agility that leads to improvement. The Japanese call this progress *kaizen*.[1] Here I will refer to it as *continuous improvement*.

RENDERING THE APPROACH VISIBLE

Every function in a company can be characterized by an image. A sales department has a conquering air, clamoring to penetrate markets, wage battles with competitors, and apply winning strategies. The research department develops new products, embodying the power of the imagination and the world of the future. The finance department evokes the mystery and allure of money, as well as the privilege of operating within an exclusive realm.

To characterize production as briefly as possible: Production is a function discussed only in response to undesirable events. "The Jackson order is delayed." "There's still too much inventory, and we'll have unsold goods left over." "There was an accident in the pressing section!" "Is the cutting line still shut down?"

When everything is going well in production, there is nothing to say.

---

[1] According to Masaaki Imai (*Kaizen*, op. cit., p. 3), the term means "ongoing improvement involving everyone, including both managers and workers. The kaizen philosophy assumes that our way of life – be it our working life, our social life, or our home life – deserves to be constantly improved." Imai stresses that kaizen is a state of mind that encourages everyone to consider it unusual when conditions do not evolve continuously. He cites a Japanese proverb: "'If a man has not been seen for three days, his friends should take a good look at him to see what changes have befallen him.' The implication is that he must have changed in three days, so his friends should be attentive enough to notice the changes." (p. 5)

An Abandoned Child

Dorothy Jongeward and Philip Seyer explain that human beings' need for recognition is so strong that if someone is deprived of opportunities to earn recognition for praiseworthy deeds, he or she may seek recognition for harmful actions. Neglected children soon develop an attitude that enables them at least to obtain unfavorable recognition: "Any reaction is better than no contact at all; any sign of recognition, even if it is unfavorable, is better than nothing!"[2]

In the factory milieu, production is often seen as the abandoned child of management. With a true cultural revolution occurring in industry, it is legitimate to ask whether the new philosophy will facilitate the recognition of production.

There are no guarantees. We must be honest: How can a person who values conformity become enthusiastic about total quality? How can someone who prefers stability become enthusiastic about just-in-time methods?

Consider plants where delays systematically accumulate at the beginning of the month until clients begin to complain. By the end of the month the delays are overcome at the price of astounding efforts.

What will people talk about on the day deadlines are met and components are well made? When the space for recognition is left empty by the reduction of these empty efforts, what favorable indicators will we fill it with?

Not every culture shows a natural readiness to accept systems of standards, as Japanese culture does. Applying standards, honoring commitments, stabilizing processes, and generally replacing the exciting eternal warfare against random factors with "peaceful" efforts that gradually banish these factors may bring profound existential anguish to some Western workplace warriors.

---

[2] Dorothy Jongeward and Philip Seyer, *Choosing Success* (New York: John Wiley and Sons, Inc., 1978).

Misguided Signs of Recognition

The problem of recognition of production has seldom been approached properly. Little can be said about a peaceful factory, but much can be said about the steps to attaining this state. Little can be said about stabilized processes, but much can be said about the extraordinary detective work necessary to discovering the many disruptive factors and finding remedies.

One error has been the orienting of indications of recognition toward results rather than toward processes that allow results to be obtained. Distinguishing between processes and results is related to a different outlook. Western firms are slowly discovering the distinction, whereas, in Japan, according to Masaaki Imai, this attitude is consistent with his nation's culture.

Imai cites many examples of daily life in Japan: For instance, the popular sumo wrestling matches award many prizes to wrestlers for the quality of their performances, even if they do not win. Likewise, at the Fushimi Inari Shrine near Kyoto, visitors must walk under 15,000 wooden *torii* (wooden gateways) before reaching the altar. Imai says, "By the time he reaches the altar, the worshipper is steeped in the sacred atmosphere of the shrine and his soul is purified. Getting there is almost as important as the prayer itself."[3]

A Medal for a Few Tea Leaves

In another example, Imai tells how servers in the cafeteria at a Matsushita plant formed a quality circle to investigate tea consumption during midday meals.

By applying precise statistical methods, carefully recording each table's consumption, and subsequently distributing teapots judiciously, they reduced tea purchases by nearly one-third. "How much were their activities worth in terms of the

---

[3] Imai, *Kaizen*, op. cit., p. 17.

actual amount of money saved? Probably very little. However, they were awarded the firm's annual presidential gold medal.[4]

The presidential medal — the most distinguished of the firm's awards — recognized the originality of these efforts in an unusual context. The result of saving a few tea leaves is meaningful only as it reveals the servers' improvement-oriented methodology. Using this methodology in the cafeteria demonstrates that collective values and methods were absorbed by every member of the plant's work force.[5]

The presidential medal honors the expansion of Matsushita's intellectual capital. If the same savings had originated from a supplier's discount, for example, the savings merely would have meant growth of the firm's financial capital.

A Widespread Problem

How can individuals who are a small fraction of a company be motivated to support the company's efforts? How can machine operators be motivated to use less oil when the savings amount to just a few hundred dollars and the firm's capital needs are stated in millions or billions of dollars?

The practices of Matsushita's president offer an answer. Merely rendering financial results visible, as with an accounting orientation, discourages people responsible for small amounts. Savings on oil are probably small. The method needed to obtain these savings, however — observation of facts, analysis, and

---

[4] Imai, *Kaizen*, op. cit., p. 20.

[5] Describing Japanese civilization, Augustin Berque cites the role of formal analogies of structures and behavior patterns in unifying a nation that is an archipelago of more than three thousand islands (*Vivre l'espace au Japon*, op. cit.).

action — closely resembles the methods senior executives apply to invest millions.[6]

Providing visibility cannot be limited merely to results. The entire approach, with a coherent sequence of phases, must be visible: the method, ideas, planning of ongoing actions, accomplishments, satisfaction, and sharing the project with the entire company.

How can the phases of visual portrayal of improvement be organized practically? The remainder of this chapter will address this question.

A TOOLBOX

Examine the document in Figure 7-1. A yellow plastic rectangle resembling a playing card, it was created at Sandouville by the Renault plant's managers to aid employees' efforts to solve production problems. Mr. Savoye, the production manager, says,

> What's written on the card isn't the only important factor. What matters is its physical existence and the fact that every employee, every technician, executive, and worker has one.
>
> When someone complains about a problem, you pull out this card, which is familiar to all, and ask 'Where do you stand in terms of method? Do you have full information about the problem? Have you analyzed probable causes? Have you talked to your coworkers about different approaches?' The card reminds people that there's a method for seeking improvement and that we all have access to it.

---

[6] Whether the scale is large or small does not matter. As an employee at Télémécanique quipped during an improvement group interview, "We're mini, but we monitor to the max."

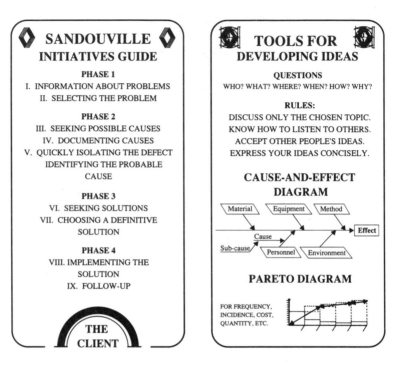

Figure 7-1. The Renault plant at Sandouville. Front and back of an "Initiatives" card.

All the members of the work force keep the cards in their pockets as a tool to use frequently. This card helps demystify "improvement" and contributes to thinking about it during daily activities.

The first message that the existence of the card conveys is that improvement does not spring from sudden inspirations. Solutions do not emerge by chance, nor are random events ordained by fate. Like everything else, improvement must be organized, and the method must be learned. Furthermore, the card's title — Tools For Developing Ideas — expresses the principle perfectly. To create a true dynamic of improvement, the workplace needs a toolbox, not just a suggestion box.

These tools have become commonplace in many firms. The rise of quality circles and other problem-solving groups has popularized data analyses and surveys, statistical processing, classification by Pareto analysis, ways to seek causes and effects, creativity techniques, and so on.

Rendering these methodological tools visible in the workplace adds a symbolic dimension. Just as displaying technical documents at work stations affirms machinists' responsibilities for manufacturing, displaying or distributing methodological documents acknowledges workers' responsibility for improvement. If a production unit's primary role — producing goods — is visible, then its secondary role — producing improvement – should likewise be visible.

CONTINUAL PROBLEM SOLVING

Among recent methods to aid group problem-solving, CEDAC merits special attention. CEDAC, which means "Cause-and-Effect Diagram with the Addition of Cards," enables groups to complete projects successfully. Its dynamism and coherence are particularly effective. Ryuji Fukuda, inventor of CEDAC, offers a description of this method in *Managerial Engineering.*[7]

CEDAC is applied in a practical context at the Simpson Timber plant near Seattle, Washington, where approximately 30 projects were in progress at the time of my visit. Charts are usually placed in work or in meeting areas. (Figure 7-2)

The charts cover various topics: improving the output of a machine for stripping bark from tree trunks, increasing the uptime availability of a saw, improving health and safety conditions, and reducing the production cycle in a specific work area.

CEDAC's distinctive feature is that it is a multifunctional tool. CEDAC promotes creativity as it provides the means of

---

[7] See Ryuji Fukuda, *Managerial Engineering* (Cambridge, Mass.: Productivity Press, 1983), and *CEDAC* (Cambridge, Mass.: Productivity Press, 1990). CEDAC is the registered service mark of Productivity, Inc.

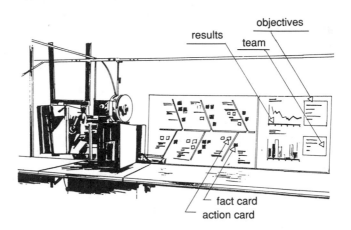

Figure 7-2. Example of CEDAC at the Simpson Timber plant near Seattle, Washington, posted near a saw to increase the machine's level of reliability.

supervising projects. These elements are combined on the same chart:

- a succinct definition of the project, including a quantified description of the initial situation and of the specified target for a set date
- identification of participants: members of the core group and the project leader
- a graph to track improvement by measuring one or more variables
- an area to record ideas under test, with the name of the person conducting the test
- an analytical framework for investigating causes

The project team posts two types of cards on the spines of the cause investigation portion of the framework. These cards can be slips of paper held on with tacks or tape, or self-sticking notes.

1. A yellow "fact card" contains data related to a specific observation about the problem under consideration. Because the CEDAC diagram is situated close to where

the problem exists, it is possible to collect a wide variety of ideas from a range of people. Thus CEDAC's concept of "facts" is broader than the concept of causes that are displayed on the traditional cause-and-effect diagram.

CEDAC cards can also be used to make observations or offer information relevant to the problem, such as correlations, specific anomalies, measurements, or hypotheses — the raw facts whose role Paul Everett stressed when he spoke to his production teams at the Simpson plant.

CEDAC cards also contain the names of the card writers and the dates. In some instances, teams take instant photographs and post them next to fact cards to provide additional information.

2. A blue "action card" or "improvement card" is placed next to one or more yellow cards. Here, too, the concept of "action" should not be confused with a final solution to the problem. It may include any corrective action or attempts to gather information or ideas to test.

Regular Meetings

Groups responsible for projects meet regularly (one hour per week at the Simpson plant) to develop new fact or action cards (usually through brainstorming), arrange the tickets, select specific actions or tests, and evaluate the status of ongoing projedts.

CEDAC is a dynamic tool placed in the locations where problems arise. Total visibility is achieved. The method is explicit, the objective is clearly identified, and results are displayed as improvement occurs.

Paul Everett, who oversees Simpson's efforts to create the basis for self-directed progress, believes that CEDAC is a powerful tool, whose use depends on careful preparation and followthrough. With proper training, however, CEDAC can become a vital resource for improvement. Says Everett, "Other people may become involved in a group's problem, even if the problem isn't theirs. Moreover, their participation is shown on the chart. The fact that operators are physically sharing the same writing medium with unit managers or technicians is also very exciting. Use of the same methodological tool, from the executive committee to production teams, helps the entire organization mobilize for launching large-scale efforts to achieve improvement. Our production units have become places where continual problem solving goes on."

When I visited the Simpson plant, an extensive project to reduce production cycles was underway using CEDAC. Instead of one chart, a series of charts was being generated, ranging from the executive committee's CEDAC, which defined major strategic aims, to production units' CEDACs, where actions were detailed. Even the marketing department had developed a CEDAC for improving the response time to the customer.

WHEN IMITATING IS PREFERABLE TO INVENTING

Continuous improvement in workplaces depends on a distinctive dynamic. Because improvement requires implementation of many practical ideas that offer prompt results without depending on revolutionary discoveries, sharing ideas plays an essential role. The desire to pursue action can arise from seeing other suggestions. An idea applied in one location can often be transposed or adapted elsewhere. In other words, imitating may be preferable to inventing.

While imparting ideas about improvements in a plant is extremely alluring, two facts must be admitted. First, the education system has poorly prepared us for labor-saving methods whose effectiveness depends on the depth of exchange.[8] Second,

---

[8] Some students readily understand the advantages of information sharing, but they come into conflict with the first commandment of academic rules – thou shalt not copy. In school such disreputable behavior would relegate them to the ranks of cheaters.

traditional modes of organization with their centralization, elitism, and compartmentalization are ill-suited for circulation of ideas.

Nevertheless, if we want factories to pursue a path of continuous improvement, changing our perspectives is absolutely necessary. Advances will occur gradually, according to management's efforts, and progress will accelerate when the results attained are visually recognizable by everyone.

Preparing the Ground

Organizing communication about improvement involves fertilizing teams' territories with ideas from other territories. Kiyoshi Suzaki evokes the need for linking "isolated islands" of production activity.[9]

This desire to promote dissemination of ideas can be observed at Mitsubishi Electric, which deploys several "Kaizen Men" in each of its plants. According to Masaaki Imai, "These are veteran blue-collar workers who have been temporarily released from their routine duties and told to roam around the plant looking for opportunities for improvement. The Kaizen-Man assignment is rotated among veteran blue-collar workers every six months or so."[10]

Companies that have successfully developed suggestion programs often publish special newsletters describing these achievements, identifying groups, and explaining solutions and methods. Inserts can also be placed inside company newsletters for each team to add to its documentation.

In general, every contact outside the original group — multidisciplinary work groups or public explanations of results — encourages dissemination of ideas.

---

[9] Suzaki, *The New Manufacturing Challenge* (New York: Free Press, 1987), p. 212-213.

[10] Imai, *Kaizen*, op. cit. p. 96.

Jean-Marie Auvinet, who oversees communications at the Sandouville Renault plant, cites a typical example of how transposition of methods can occur within organizations. After attending a meeting on reducing setup time in production units, Auvinet became inspired. For events that needed specific technical support (audiovisual materials, charts, rearrangement of seats), he adopted the time-study method being applied in production units. He halved the amount of time needed to prepare the lecture room.

A Forum to Expand Dialogue

The Renault plant at Sandouville hold monthly forums. At these meetings, working groups explain project results to management representatives, with audiovisual support. Apart from material and cultural benefits — recognition for teams, pride in working at a plant where improvement is occurring — these events allow ideas to circulate among departments. Everyone gains something. The people describing projects must formally describe their experiences, and their listeners can discover methods being applied elsewhere.

Most important, everyone learns from actual experiences. "When I leave the meeting," one of the participants explains, "I'm truly convinced about what's possible. I have only one wish: to do the same thing."

AN IDEA EXCHANGE

At the Renault Sandouville plant, an *Idea Exchange*[11] has replaced the suggestion box. Is there a more symbolic way to evoke sharing of ideas? A system of bonuses for suggestions

---

[11] The French term is *Bourse aux Idées*, which means "stock exchange of ideas," a place where people can exchange their ideas with other people's.

had existed for several years, but involved slow and selective written procedures (not everyone is comfortable completing documents). Hence, the Idea Exchange was created alongside the bonus system, which remains in use for suggestions at some levels. The Idea Exchange is now being tested in one of the plant's departments.

Elements of the Idea Exchange

- The Idea Exchange is ideal for ideas that can be applied easily. The implementation period should not exceed one week. Completion of documentation is not required and administrative procedures are confined to a small group.
- A budget is provided for the unit, which completes transactions directly with local firms to implement suggestions.
- Suggestions are limited to a specific thematic area. Every six months, a new theme is defined by management: introduction of a new vehicle, a quality campaign, reduction of costs for materials, and so on.
- Specific measures render the exchange of ideas visible. Green stickers are attached to a chart placed near the indicators chart. (Figure 7-3) The numbers of stickers for group members matches their numbers of suggestions. A unit log records suggestions, and a curve plotted on the indicator chart monitors changes in the number of suggestions.
- Every applicable idea (the appropriate supervisory personnel decide what is applicable) is rewarded with points. Each team member receives a notebook to record his or her points. After earning a certain number of points, team members can exchange them for incentive merchandise. Initially, there was a list, but the project now uses a system of purchasing vouchers. The number of points for every idea is ten, regardless of the value of

Figure 7-3. Chart for recording improvement ideas implemented by the team. Stickers are placed next to each member's name to account for their ideas.

the idea. This principle reduces complicated computations. If an idea is potentially more far-reaching, a file is created for it in the bonus-based suggestion system.

How the Exchange Works

The number of points does not depend on the potential financial value of suggestions to the company. This innovative system places value instead on collaboration.

For example, if four people cooperate to find a solution for a problem, each of them earns ten points. If an employee develops an idea about a process that is the focus of another person's work, the first employee must involve the other person and convince him or her that the idea is valid. If the first person successfully sells the idea, each of them can earn ten points.

The same principle is adopted for cooperation between day shift and evening shift teams. If a team member manages to convince a coworker of the validity of his or her idea, each of them earns ten points.

The basic principles of the Idea Exchange embody dissemination and exchanging of ideas. "A machinist who wishes to sell an idea to other units is encouraged to," says Mr. Lebrun, a technical assistant who manages the project. "If a given idea can be applied in 18 areas, the machinist earns 180 points and enables those who have made the effort to participate in the proposal to earn together 180 points."

Project Development

The project was developed by a group of units that constituted a pilot group. "People became involved quickly," Mr. Lebrun said. The basic concept seemed simple, and they were especially gratified that ideas would be applied rapidly. At the outset, one skeptic said, 'I bet your rewards are made in Japan.' After observing his coworkers' participation for a while, he felt left out. Now, he's the one with the highest point total."

After the project was launched, it was necessary to publicize it. The working group produced a videotape in which each participant explains the function of the Idea Exchange. The videotape is for viewing on monitors in other units, so everyone can understand the project.

DISPLAYING SCHEDULES FOR CURRENT ENDEAVORS

A firm that adopts a goal of continuous improvement must seek in-depth solutions for a vast number of small problems that may once have been approached superficially. On the long march toward zero defects or zero breakdowns, a series of obstacles of all kinds emerges that must be overcome. Simultaneous management of a large number of projects at multiple locations in the plant becomes necessary.

Schedules or plans for these projects should be visible in work areas, for two reasons. First, placing schedules in work areas directly conveys that work areas are now involved in improvement projects. These projects are no longer the domain of the research office or the operations department. Now these projects relate to everyone, from those who operate production tools to those who provide technical assistance.

The symbolic power of displayed information has been evoked. Displaying collective commitments in a work area helps mobilize the group for action.[12]

Practical benefits also result. The act of placing a project monitoring chart where many people pass by significantly affects the promptness of results. This acceleration occurs because concealing problems is difficult when anyone entering the area can see red stickers accumulating on the schedule for weeks. (Figure 7-4)

When everyone can see, it is impossible to close one's eyes. Powerful group dynamic develops that impels the entire organization toward action.

HIGHLIGHTING ACCOMPLISHMENTS

Consider Figure 7-5, which shows a machine tool at the Citroën plant in Caen. In the front portion, a panel displays a "PQG" logo, which stands for "Product Quality Guaranteed." This emblem is placed on every machine included in a study coordinated by the production team. Their goal is to improve the quality of processes by installing mistake-proofing devices (known as *poka-yoke* in Japan).

---

[12] Announcing that a production unit's problems are everyone's concern does not mean conferring obligations imprecisely. A coordinator is appointed to oversee the process. This person's name is indicated on the chart. (Figure 7-4) The idea of shared responsibility means that everyone who influences results at all should consider himself or herself involved until a solution is developed.

Problem	Week number	Project leader/ extension
Flange specifications	●●●○	MF/201
Balancing the line	●●●●●○	NG/504
Paint flow rate	●○	JG/171
Work station prep	●●●●●●●●●●○	TW/614

● = Solution sought   ● = Solution being developed   ○ = Problem solved

Figure 7-4. The Renault Sandouville plant. Schedule of current activities, displayed in a work area. There are many models for a chart of this kind. The purpose of the chart is to facilitate communication. It should be simple and understandable at a glance. Additional information can be provided on another document.

Figure 7-5. The Citroën plant in Caen. A placard indicates installation of a mistake-proofing device (*poka-yoke*) on a machine.

The intention behind this marking is to provide more visibility for quality efforts. This visibility is necessary, for the hundreds of small advances alone are often undramatic. A robotized or a highly sophisticated galvanizing system can be seen, whereas the installation of a clever device for reducing omitted components may go unnoticed.

While a graph of changes in a quality indicator is also a suitable way to express progress, this type of information alone is insufficient. First, on a comprehensive graph the benefits of an error-prevention device might be offset by the negative impact of other problems. Second, improvement is no longer observable shortly after it is expressed as a curve on a chart. A decrease in the level of defective items is confirmed, and no one thinks about it again.

On the other hand, when accomplishments are announced, everyone passing by can say, "That unit isn't sitting on its hands." With a commemorative marker, the group's efforts remain visibly confirmed.

One question often arises concerning this type of identification: Should the names of idea originators appear on the placards? In my experience, this measure is not desirable, for two reasons.

First, recognizing sources of ideas is always delicate with collective endeavors. A nameless display allows all members of the work group to take pride as originators.

Second, visual communication allows exceptional diversity in transmission of messages. This diversity can be used advantageously. Messages pertaining to objects should be the only messages appearing on a given item, so that acknowledgment of facts is detached from acknowledgment for individuals. In this way, the identity of the territory is reinforced, and, newcomers can be absorbed more rapidly.[13] We will examine individual recognition at a later point.

---

[13] The team's name can be recorded, however. Identifying a team is not equivalent to naming its members. Recording the team name on a designation for improvements is not a barrier to the absorption of newcomers.

Practical Requirements

The visual display of improvements can be extended to many areas: a machine that is to be involved in systematic preventive maintenance, a work station with self-monitoring, a lifting system outfitted with a safety device, or a trimming machine with reduced waste levels. In some instances, attaching a sticker symbolizing a current process (total quality plan, just-in-time, and so on) is enough. In other cases, detailed posters can be provided that describe improvements and financial advantages. (Figures 7-6 and 7-7)

Complicated methods for calling attention to changes are not needed. As in Chapter 3, the fact of placing dates on displayed operating standards in a highly visible form allows the measurement of improvement. Before-and-after photographs are also used in many cases. (Figure 7-8)

Quantity Matters

The chief executive officer of a company is unlikely to congratulate the head of the research department for submitting a large number of investment projects. The CEO would be more keenly interested in financial criteria such as rates of return, or recovery periods.

The principle of making a continuous-improvement indicator dependent on quantity instead of on profitability constitutes a sharp break with the traditional economic approach. A firm begins to prefer one hundred suggestions that can yield $25 apiece, instead of one suggestion that can yield $2500. The nature of continuous improvement explains this attitude:

- The largest possible number of people should adopt the concept of improvement. Once adopted, the process will become an aspect of the company's culture.

Figure 7-6. The Citroën plant, Caen. A panel describes an improvement introduced in a work area, indicating the amount saved. The panel hangs above the location of the procedure.

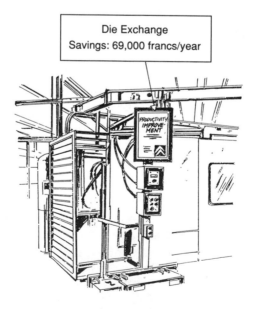

Die Exchange
Savings: 69,000 francs/year

Figure 7-7. The Citroën plant, Caen. Increases in a machine's productivity as a result of a significant reduction in the changeover time.

- Continuous improvement is sustained by its own momentum. When members of production teams observe that it is possible to obtain concrete results quickly, their perceptions of their environment change immediately. Team members begin to observe more attentively. They recognize that they can perform better and acquire greater self-confidence as well as become interested in other teams' activities. From then on, they generate ideas about improvements.

The plant enters a stage that Mr. Leichle, manager of the Bendix plant in Toulouse, refers to as "spontaneous motion toward improvement." The quantity of ideas, instead of their intrinsic merit, makes it possible to attain the critical mass for natural expansion of progress.

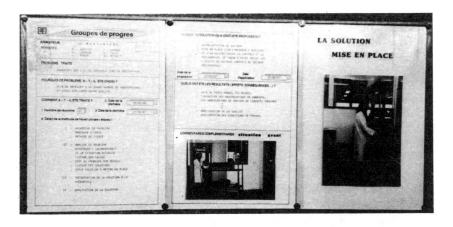

Figure 7-8. A work area display at the Télémécanique plant at Carros. The written panels describe the team's project (an improved method of transporting integrated circuits to save time and handling and improve quality). The middle photo shows the method before improvement (carts) and the right shows the implemented solution (a conveyor).

Figure 7-9. At the Renault Sandouville plant. Large yellow and black stripes have been painted on the floor area cleared by reducing the inventory of bumpers near an assembly line. Thus, until the area is reassigned for production, a twofold advantage has been obtained: There is no longer a risk of the area being inundated with parts, and everyone can observe a symbolic representation of progress in keeping with the plant's just-in-time project. Furthermore, this open floorspace is no longer regarded as a cost charged to the production unit.

AN IMPROVEMENT RECORD

The Hewlett-Packard plant in Fort Collins, Colorado, establishes a Problem-Solving Storyboard file when a working group assumes responsibility for a problem. (Figure 7-11) As soon as efforts to solve a problem begin, a file is begun at the same location as the problem. According to Dan Blount, a manufacturing engineering manager, this practice offers three advantages:

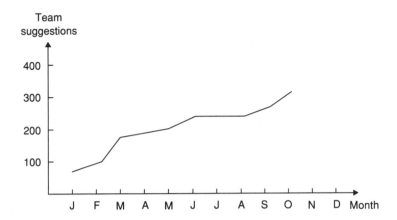

Figure 7-10. The Hewlett-Packard plant at Fort Collins, Colorado. A curve charting team members' suggestions that have been applied. This graph is displayed outside the office of the supervisor for the production unit. The number of suggestions contributed by employees is one of the criteria management uses to evaluate supervisors.

- First, the standard nature of the files enables groups to seek proper methodological development of required phases. Each stage is clearly identified. New employees can easily learn the method, step by step.
- Second, when a problem is solved, the file is placed near the production line. Thus, files are available for anyone to consult, so that similar problems that other production teams discover can be solved. The engineering department also finds it beneficial for files pertaining to problems encountered in recent years to be available in the workplace.
- Last, the presence of files in the location where a process occurs is symbolically important. These improvement records demonstrate to newcomers that each production unit possesses a history, even a turbulent one.

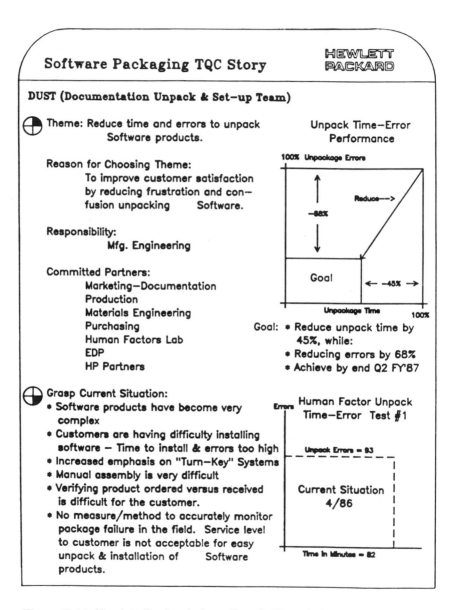

Figure 7-11. Hewlett-Packard plant, Fort Collins, Colorado. Problem solving storyboard.

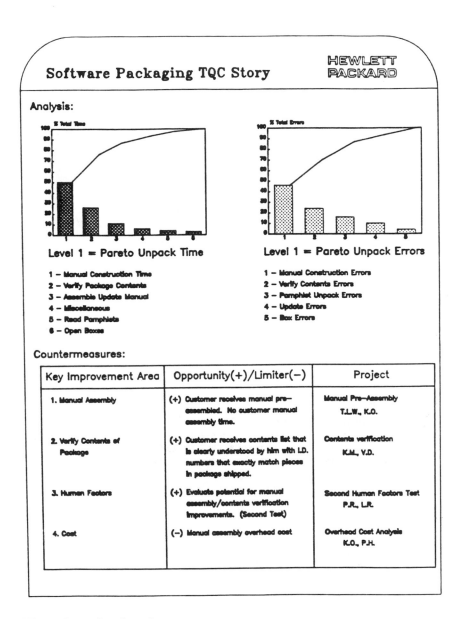

Software Packaging TQC Story

HEWLETT PACKARD

Analysis:

Level 1 = Pareto Unpack Time

1 — Manual Construction Time
2 — Verify Package Contents
3 — Assemble Update Manual
4 — Miscellaneous
5 — Read Pamphlets
6 — Open Boxes

Level 1 = Pareto Unpack Errors

1 — Manual Construction Errors
2 — Verify Contents Errors
3 — Pamphlet Unpack Errors
4 — Update Errors
5 — Box Errors

Countermeasures:

Key Improvement Area	Opportunity(+)/Limiter(−)	Project
1. Manual Assembly	(+) Customer receives manual pre-assembled. No customer manual assembly time.	Manual Pre-Assembly T.L.W., K.O.
2. Verify Contents of Package	(+) Customer receives contents list that is clearly understood by him with I.D. numbers that exactly match pieces in package shipped.	Contents verification K.M., V.D.
3. Human Factors	(+) Evaluate potential for manual assembly/contents verification improvements. (Second Test)	Second Human Factors Test P.R., L.R.
4. Cost	(−) Manual assembly overhead cost	Overhead Cost Analysis K.O., P.H.

(Figure 7-11. Continued)

Software Packaging TQC Story

HEWLETT
PACKARD

 Check Effectiveness:

Analysis (A)
Second Human Factors Test prototype
improvements for manual pre—assembly
and contents verification lists.

Results:
* Error reduction = −83%
* Time reduction = −50%

Analysis (B)
Evaluation of prototype manual pre—assy

Results:
* Re—layout of software production area
  required to improve JIT & mtl handling

Analysis (C)
Manual assembly production cost:

Results:
* 16% increase in manual assembly overhead costs

100% Unpackage Errors

Reduce—>

− 83%

Goal

Actual

<—+ −50%—>

Unpackage Time   100%
Second Human Factors Test − 12/86

 Action/Standardization (Q1, Q2 FY'87)

(A) Implement manual pre—assembly process in Q1 FY'87
(B) Re—layout production area to optimize JIT material flow and handling
    and include manual pre—assembly in Q1 FY'87
(C) Implement on—line customer contents verification lists in Q2 FY'87
(D) Establish field failure rate process in Q1 FY'87, collect results in Q1
    and Q2 and set goal for FFR reduction by end of Q2 for FY'87

 Future Action/Residual Problems (Q3, Q4 FY'87)

(A) Develop in—process measurements of quality & identify Process TQC
    improvements
(B) Develop umbrella TQC project to facilitate continuing improvement

(Figure 7-11. Continued)

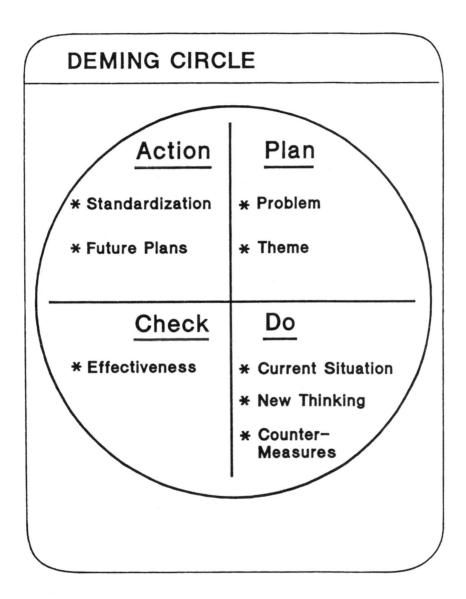

(Figure 7-11. Continued)

On joining the group — even for two or three months —
each new member discovers the opportunity to leave a trace of
his or her presence in an improvement record.[14]

VISIBLE SATISFACTION

When suggestion boxes were fashionable, it seemed
important for those who contributed ideas to receive bonuses
computed according to the anticipated gains. Limiting recognition to a financial incentive was a mistake, characterized by
three problems.

First, a financial incentive can promote artificial interest in
the process. A project that can quickly offer some money easily
gains enthusiastic participation. This kind of ease, however, dis-
suades an organization from undertaking the necessary
preparatory efforts to incorporate a improvement-oriented
methodology in its activities.

Second, because special bonuses may be added to wages as
compensation for ideas, people will feel that they are not normally paid for thinking. How then is it possible to affirm
improvement as an integral part of ordinary functions?

Finally, a third problem: How can a proportional bonus
encourage people with modest ideas, or skilled observers who
are not creators, or those who offer only a part of a solution?
This kind of bonus cannot encourage teamwork. Above all, a
bonus can encourage people to keep valuable observations to
themselves, whereas improvement is obtained through cross-
fertilization, comparison, and sharing of ideas.

These circumstances do not mean that rewards are to no
avail. Rewards, however, must be transformed or modified by

---

[14] Once again, visual organization of the workplace reinforces territorial identification. The development of an official "territorial" history, which cannot
be reduced to the centralized history of the company itself, is a recent phenomenon in factory life.

factors other than the financial, although they should have some symbolic value in the domain of communication. Rewards must be integrated with ordinary experiences.

At Fleury Michon, members of quality circles are interviewed by the in-house video magazine producer when they finish a project. In the video magazine, quality circle members describe the problems they overcame, the methods they applied, and the results they obtained, as they stand near a machine or a work station. In the United States, I have often seen large boards at entrances to work areas, with photographs of teams that have achieved significant advances. (Figure 7-12)

All forms of recognition that can reinforce solidarity within a group or mark its identity are appreciated. At the J. Reydel plant in Gondecourt, a team that had achieved its objectives

Figure 7-12. Gorman Rupp plant, Mansfield, Ohio. At this pump manufacturer, congratulations are posted at the entrance to a work area for a project to which the entire team contributed. On the right are photographs of the employees who did the job.

enjoyed a large cake decorated with a candy replica of the product manufactured in the team's work area. At the Valeo plant near Le Mans, when a large project was completed, the production manager arranged a visit to a client's plant for a group of machinists.

In every instance, the form of recognition that is most meaningful to the originator of a suggestion is to be allowed to participate in its implementation. Even if his or her involvement may be limited to explaining or monitoring certain phases, the originator should maintain contact with the department that applies the suggestion. The originator should be informed about improvement and should be able to visit the people implementing the suggestion to offer opinions at certain vital points. Observing a process that implements our own ideas can be one of the strongest inducements to developing new ideas.[15]

Letters from the Heart

France Abonnements processes thousands of magazine subscription files every day, including inquiries about magazines that did not arrive or changes of address. "At a certain point," Michele Pilhan indicates, "these inquiries led to an adversarial state of mind. Employees came to regard clients as perpetual malcontents."

This manager ingeniously transformed the elements of the problem by promoting a personalized relationship between the processing department and clients. The goal was for correspondence, instead of being conducted adversarially, to create an

---

[15] The satisfaction of doing a good job is what Jim Heckel, production manager at Hewlett-Packard's plant in Greeley, Colorado, had in mind when he mentioned a new improvement indicator. This indicator, he explained, is often overlooked in companies, and a way of calculating it has never been described in books about investment theory. This indicator is ROSE, or Return on Self Esteem. Experts are now giving it a prominent position beside ROI (Return on Investment).

opportunity for employees to establish a favorable relationship with clients. Thus correspondence from a particular client would always be handled by the same person. Some letters would receive handwritten replies, prepared and signed by the employee responsible for managing the particular file.

"At first, I hoped that they would soon give me a type-writer," said an employee responsible for correspondence. "Then, after a certain period of time, clients began to write to me and thank me in person. Many times these were very moving letters, written by ordinary people who had been touched by my letters."

Every day a board at the entrance to the processing center in Chantilly displays a different letter from a satisfied client. (Figure 7-13) When employees arrive in the morning, the first thing they do is go to the board to read the letter. At France Abonnements, this correspondence is known as "letters from the heart."[16]

Figure 7-13. Entrance to the France Abonnements processing center in Chantilly.

---

[16] This is a translation of "Le courrier du coeur," the name given to personal correspondence and advice columns in French newspapers.

A JOINT PROJECT

Declaring intentions to provide better service for customers, appealing to employees to prevent waste, proclaiming the crusade for total quality: These are all fashionable ideas. Rapid dissemination of these ideas is becoming a trend.

Displays about general themes are easy to prepare. It is more difficult to ensure that written material will not be contradicted every day by actual experiences. Drafting a text about respect for the individual is not enough to eradicate the authoritarianism of leadership. Displaying a poster proclaiming that quality is a priority objective is not enough to reorient an organization obsessed with producing greater quantities.

With visual communication, whatever the observer sees is endowed with meaning. Visual communication's effectiveness is attributable to the fact that it contributes to development of a coherent image of the world. If there is any contradiction between the contents of a chart and the realities an observer sees every day, visual communication loses its power. Charts may be present physically in work areas, but they become psychologically invisible.

This fundamental requirement of creating coherent visual discourse throughout a plant prompted me to defer examining more general themes until the end of this book. Companies should respect the same principle. Before putting up improvement charts, post instructions. Before announcing a project on posters, place maintenance schedules near the machines — and respect them. Before declaring that the entire organization will adhere to lofty values, make sure you have swept the work areas.

Visual communication is a new language, and to learn it requires effort. It is impossible to write prose before learning grammar.

A Pyramid in Colorado

The number of companies that attempt to keep all of their employees informed about major company projects is extremely small. This is true especially if the company considers a major project as one that affects the technical and organizational context of a company's employees: new products, technological development, and large-scale investment.

When I advise companies to provide better information for their employees, I hear: "They aren't interested in that. We put out a memo, but no one read it." Of course — who wants to read memoranda? Try a more dynamic and stimulating mode of communication. Digital Equipment Corporation's example demonstrates that with a suitable effort it is possible to depart from customary paths.

In 1986, DEC decided to modify the computer system that managed production at its Colorado Springs plant. The ramifications of such a project can affect the entire work force of a plant. The success of the project, therefore, depends on its widespread acceptance.

One day, about two months after the project had begun, everyone who went to lunch was surprised by a pyramid. (Figure 7-14) A magnificent, well-proportioned structure of painted plywood had been mounted on a stand in the middle of the cafeteria. The same small rectangles were present on each side, each one representing a computer software package. The names of each package had been recorded, with the anticipated date for its release. When a package was ready, the corresponding area was colored with a felt-tipped highlighter. On completion of the project, the rectangles would reach to a small American flag mounted at the peak.

Figure 7-14. A six foot pyramid at Digital Equipment Corporation, Colorado Springs. The darkened squares represent installed software packages. The coloring is transparent so that the names of packages in use can still be read.

During the year the project lasted, this way to portray the schedule was highly effective. Because the schedule was visible in a public area, the computerization project was understood as everyone's concern. Each employee was in contact with the project and hoped that it would be completed on schedule. Because many employees were fascinated with the expanding red areas, the team handling the implementation was often approached for information about a given package or about difficulties hindering application.

Because the project group felt that it was being observed by everyone, it was eager to demonstrate that it could complete its tasks within the specified period. So completely did the pyramid transform the schedule into a thing of universal concern that no one was able to tell me who had first proposed it.

Seeing a Mission Statement

A mission statement is more far-reaching than a project, expressing principles that a company has selected to pursue as its future. A mission statement contributes to identifying a system of values and to strengthening a collective identity.

There are many visual ways to present messages, and I will discuss some of them later. A preparatory phase is always necessary. A mission statement should first be discussed in meetings or during training. The endeavor requires multiple explanations, because time is needed for a consensus to develop. A mission statement is only useful if each member of the organization believes that it expresses his or her beliefs.

At the Renault plant, a mobile display stand was sent from one work area to another before a mission statement for the assembly division was announced. Promotion of the mission statement was aided by a ten-minute videotape prepared by a task force to explain the basis of the statement and the significance of written messages.

One way to facilitate the assimilation process is to allow for the visualization of a mission statement on two levels. The first level involves a general document, issued by a company's management and discussed throughout the firm. The second level involves production units or teams. In this way, the format of the mission statement can be adapted individually. (Figure 7-15)

The process of adapting a general text to a specific framework is an excellent way to understand its meaning. In a situation where the form must be changed, a group discovers the substance of the mission statement. A firm's resources and diversity are more fully revealed by the group of derived documents than if the original had been replicated.

Mission statements can have various physical embodiments — a playing card, a document for new employees, or posters in work areas. The use of one medium does not exclude others.

To place a mission statement in a document for individual use is also a suitable way to promote its acceptance. In some cases, the mission statement can be printed in a small address book. Some firms give small booklets to employees at the beginning of the year. The firm's general policies appear on the first page. The second page is completed by the plant manager, who states the particular plant's objectives. The third page is reserved for the unit supervisor to define his or her own policies in relation to the preceding pages. The fourth page indicates the practical measures needed for advancing in the proper direction. Thus, general ideas are transformed into concrete intentions. The company's policies cease to be an abstraction; they become a reality for everyone.

Figure 7-15. The Omark plant in Oroville, California, which manufactures hunting equipment. A company statement painted on a wall by a team.

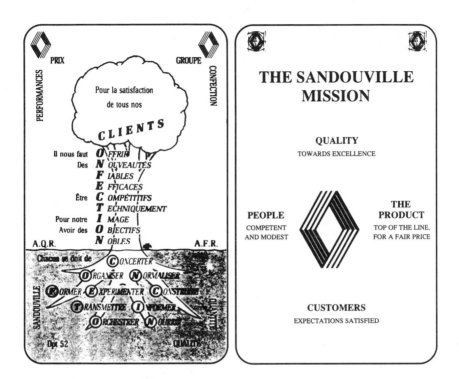

Figure 7-16. At the Renault Sandouville plant, the playing-card format is popular. Initially, a single card was created for the entire plant. Later, each department developed its own card. With two sides of the cards, the mission statement for the entire plant appears on one side and the department's principles on the other. The department side is left untranslated to show an acrostic of the department's name ("Confection") used to identify its principles.

**The Ten
Commandments
of Mercure**

• Drastically reduce production lead time.

• Track down waste.

• Encourage order, neatness, and precision.

• Invest continuously in productivity.

• Transform the layout to speed the flow.

• Allow operators to guarantee their quality.

• Expand use of mistake-proofing devices to help people.

• Value feasibility over technical achievement.

• Develop simple and dependable methods.

• Subdivide production in autonomous cells and expand

to a global approach.

Onward Citroën !

Figure 7-17. The Citroën plant, Caen. Card with a mission statement for
"Mercure," the company's long-term quality project.

8

Implementing Visual Communication

When I invited the reader on this journey through visual factories, my intention was to offer practical recommendations, examples, and a guide for contemplating an especially evocative mode of communication.

When you are ready to initiate action, however, you may be perplexed by what you have read here. On one hand, the physical preparation of visual media does not appear to pose problems. On the other hand, this apparent ease may conceal difficulty in successfully introducing visual communication. Awareness of these difficulties should persuade us to be prudent and avoid launching projects without conducting a careful planning phase.

But how should this form of deliberation be pursued? Must one path be followed to apply the ideas described within this book? Where do we begin? How far can we go?

By observing the plants that have been successful in using visual communication, we realize that we must reject the idea of a sole approach. Rather, there is an amazing diversity of applications.

This diversity springs from the close relationship between visual organization and a given firm's culture. Like individuals, no two factories possess the same face.

In terms of ways to create a visual organization project, remember that the firms I visited demonstrated significant flexibility. At the same time, however, this pragmatism respected certain general conditions in creating a suitable human and organization context for success. While not a detailed set of instructions, here are five recommended guidelines for successful applications:

- Establish goals for the project.
- Determine the need for changes in culture.
- Establish a comprehensive plan.
- Create the need.
- Ensure the implementation.

ESTABLISHING GOALS FOR A PROJECT

If we surveyed a firm's executives about the factors that induced them to develop communication involving the display of data and messages, the responses would sound like: "This will let everyone be informed at the same time." "It's like advertising; it has a strong impact." "Keeping up with your own results always provides motivation."

While not incorrect, these replies are insufficient. In this book we have seen that beyond the appearance of various media, visual communication relies on a specific mode of organization, *visual organization*.

I have emphasized that this mode of organization permits the strengthening of a given plant along several strategic axes:

- *Improving flexibility of production resources:* expanding employees' autonomy in their relationships with machines and their environment; developing mobility and versatility within teams.

- *Contributing to introduction of decentralization policies:* developing simple visual decision-making systems (visual production control, monitoring of machines and processes).
- *Greater production efficiency:* eliminating some of the intermediate functions of supervisory personnel, reorienting them toward functions of organization, team leadership, and technical assistance.
- *Accelerated solution of workplace problems:* mobilizing production teams to observe and analyze anomalies and difficulties.
- *Greater integration within an organization:* simultaneous reinforcement of teams' internal cohesion and their relations with the rest of the firm; intensified exchanges, improved dialogue among operational departments, enrichment of contacts with clients and suppliers, greater involvement in the firm's overall policies.

This list demonstrates how the advantages of visual organization far exceed the ordinary benefits of an information system. But it would be a pity for a firm to launch a project — which is not easy to pursue successfully — without initially defining a guiding perspective for the project. Is it merely a matter of introducing posters recommending that people wear safety shoes or proclaiming that quality is everyone's concern? Or is the objective to achieve more effective management through visual communication?

If the first hypothesis is valid, the process involves few difficulties, but offers little possibility to produce impressive results. If the second hypothesis is adopted, then the scale of the project is entirely different. Intentions must be expressed clearly; everyone must know the firm's intended orientation from the outset.

In this phase of defining objectives, the firm's steering committee must participate, playing a dual role. First, before the initial attempts at implementation, the committee is responsible for defining the company's expectations of visual communication and how visual communication will contribute to the success of the firm's manufacturing policies.

Second, the steering committee must determine whether the company's culture is prepared to accept specific elements of visual communication. The committee must also decide on the necessary measures for adaptation of the program.

DETERMINING THE NEED FOR CULTURAL CHANGES

When I mentioned the paradox of calling "revolutionary" a mode of communication that is several thousand years old, I also observed how strange it was that factories used visual communication so infrequently. This reluctance springs from a conflict between traditional company culture and approaches that use an open mode of communication.

Company rules that forbid employees to chat with their neighbors, to leave their work stations without permission, or to whistle while they work are steadily lessening. Nevertheless, the attitudes that engender rules of this kind are still alive in many places.

Clearly, it is fruitless to introduce a visual organization project without measuring the distance that must be covered on a cultural plane.

The principal components of the visual communication are the following:

- Placing knowledge and information in the *public domain*
- Enabling the ownership of the environment by its occupants (*territory*)
- Enabling users to participate in creating *rules and standards*
- Increasing the amount of work done by *small groups*
- Increasing *informal contact* outside of the hierarchy

- Developing a system of *overlapping responsibilities*, especially among production departments and functional departments (maintenance, facilities, industrial engineering, and so on)
- Reorienting inspection functions toward *observation of facts and problem-solving*, instead of monitoring individuals and seeking to blame
- The participation of production personnel in *improvement projects* in the workplace
- *Returning to the shop-floor level* after years of centralized management
- *Returning to reality* after years of management by abstractions

Because visual communication embodies such a decisive break with tradition, these ten points are tantamount to a cultural revolution. Must we conclude that a firm not satisfying these ten requirements is incapable of adopting visual communication?

A qualified answer is necessary. On one hand, all visual workplaces are committed to this visual orientation. Yet, in many plants visual communication is successful, although this level of culture change has not been precisely attained. Multiple levels of progress are inherent to these types of projects. Advancing from an attitude of hoarding to an attitude of sharing information does not happen overnight. The important requirement is for management and supervisory personnel to support the sharing of information while communicating their beliefs to the entire company.

Here are two recommendations:

- Never start a visual communication project without first verifying the company's commitment to the path defined by the principles cited above. Visual communication should never be approached purely as technique.

If a firm's central management does not uphold this concept, displaying of information will not advance beyond gimmicks and lip service. Boards placed in work areas will merely serve as public evidence of a bungled policy of openness, until someone removes them.

- On the other hand, the company does not need to complete each stage leading to the cultural ideal before it displays graphs for the first time. Once the first barriers of the relationship between authority and possession of information have been removed, it is possible to start.

Beyond the starting point, visual communication becomes a true ally of the cultural project because of its ability to stimulate dialogue and overcome hierarchical barriers.

Visual communication cannot flourish without certain attitudes. At the same time, however, it contributes to the development of these attitudes. Thus, the content of a project is reinforced through its implementation. The important aspect is to believe in the project and to begin.

ESTABLISHING A COMPREHENSIVE PLAN

A company's mission statement in a notebook, a warning light on a machine, storage areas traced on the floor, a photograph of a recent improvement in equipment introduced by a quality circle — when listed together, these media make a surreal inventory. These features of a visual landscape share certain points, however. The systematic use of these items reflects a distinctive relationship between human beings and the *semiosphere*, which consists of all of the signs that appear within a given environment. This relationship does not merely belong to the domain of the appearance of the place; rather, it corresponds to the rise of an actual language that is specific to developing collective and decentralized organizational structures.

If management accepts this proposition, modifications of the visual environment naturally must be based on a concept of the path that the plant will ultimately follow and an overview of areas that are susceptible to transformation.

Nevertheless, despite the usefulness of a comprehensive plan, a managerial approach should not be adopted that relies on an authoritarian mode of implementation. Doing so creates a conflict with the nature of visual organization, whose development must consider the needs that are actually identifiable in the workplace.

Thus management must create a framework and delineate orientations rather than define a detailed program. This framework allows the most effective synergy among different themes, using favorable circumstances that may arise in a work area and disseminating solutions throughout the company.

All actions must occur within the context of a coherent vision. Initial preparation, training, adaptation of a firm's culture, the ability to assimilate messages, and all of the many efforts undertaken to launch a project will justify themselves in the long-term results.

Diagnosis

Diagnosis should precede the development of any plan. A diagnosis developed in reference to categories I have discussed reveals the strengths and weaknesses of available communication resources in a workplace.

After diagnosis, entrust a research group with the task of defining principal orientations according to the desired objectives. The research group should include the firm's principal executives.

There is no universal answer to the question of knowing where to begin. Nevertheless, here are two recommendations:

- Begin to develop visual organization from its foundation rather than its superstructure. Establishing a *territory* (identification, planning of areas for specific functions, establishing order, neatness) is part of the foundation, along with creation of *visual documentation* (standards, methods, knowledge). Components of the superstructure include the operational themes discussed earlier: flow and inventory control, monitoring production, indicators and improvement.

- With operational themes, allot priority to the ones that offer the greatest likelihood of success. A cultural dimension that offers a responsive milieu exists in relation to every act of visual communication. It is useless to begin in a domain where the risks of failure are high. For example, a plant where monitoring performance levels leads to frequent conflict about wages will find it difficult to introduce the display of indicators quickly. A firm that has not mastered its own logistical structure cannot afford to display delivery goals that are constantly unmet.

The entire organization needs to discover the advantages of visual organization from the outset. The most vital task is to furnish evidence that it works.

Expansion to Other Departments

Within this book, I have intentionally restricted my scrutiny of visual organization to the domain of manufacturing. Nevertheless, it is difficult to initiate activities in production units while leaving the rest of a company untouched.

For management to proceed in this way, it would be perceived as speaking with two tongues. Can management praise the advantages of total visibility while encouraging some units to become far more visual than others?

Acknowledging general attributes of visual organization, applications need not be limited to one unit. Most of the examples cited are readily transferable to technical departments, administrative units, sales divisions, and to any context where work is performed collectively.

By initiating projects in sectors other than production units, a company can improve the likelihood of success of the visual project. Thus projects can be situated on the only appropriate foundation: the cultural foundation of the company.

CREATING THE NEED

I have emphasized the need for an ownership process while conducting a visual organization project. Among the factors that contribute to the successful development of this process, a vital element is a perceived need on the part of users.

For example, assume that a friend has offered you a tool to perform various jobs. If you use the tool frequently, you may soon begin to call it "my tool." On the other hand, if you never find a practical use, you will not visualize it as a tool. Its image will continue to be abstract. Like an unwanted gift, the tool inside its wrappings will merely evoke the generous (but out-of-touch) giver's intentions.

A similar situation exists in the workplace. Physical media are packaging, whereas the information that can be extracted from them constitutes a tool. When a visual communication project is initiated, an early goal must be to stimulate the user's wish to remove the tool from its wrappings.

In practical terms, a visual medium should never appear to be a goal *per se*; instead, it must be seen as the most appropriate means of solving a problem. One should never produce boards, install signals, or provide televisions in work areas without having created conditions that render their presence useful.

For example, instill a desire for improvement in production teams before displaying performance indicators. Before developing visual documentation, establish conditions of autonomy that ask for reinforcement of methodological rigorousness. Before displaying programs or schedules in workplaces, redefine responsibilities in terms of planning.

Likewise, if the situation involves displaying panels that indicate a production unit's activities or team members' identities, make this step respond to a need: the start of a new team activity, contact with the external world (plant visits, open door days), launching of company projects, and so on.

The element that should receive priority attention in a visual information project is the *question* rather than the *answer*. You cannot sell visual information to customers who are incapable of understanding its value.

By proceeding in this manner, a plant can protect itself from a greater risk: converting visual communication into a merely cosmetic process. In raising questions about the factors that create a need for information, it is impossible to avoid a deep and coherent reflection. By asking questions one avoids initiating efforts only half-way, like the plant that displayed charts indicating results, but failed to allow sufficient time for employees to read and to discuss them.

ENSURING THE IMPLEMENTATION

The time to take action has arrived. *Think big, start small* is a frequently heard recommendation. "Thinking big" is done in the preparatory phases. "Starting small" is what counts at the point of committing to action.

Introducing visual media throughout an entire plant all at once may prove difficult. Different production units may not have the same culture. Bear this point in mind in terms of selecting appropriate times and locations.

Assimilation is a process that requires time. Unduly rapid introduction of visual media may endow a project with an authoritarian aura that becomes an obstacle to success.

When themes, locations, and times have been chosen, pragmatism should prevail with implementation. The important objective is to see concrete results quickly. When a production unit begins to transmit visual messages, other employees will visit it. The desire to do the same (and to do better) emerges naturally. Initial attempts can create favorable conditions for the entire organization.

Do Not Seek Perfection

Seeking to obtain flawless results too quickly is also useless. A prototypical chart, a provisional display method, or a simple contrivance may facilitate assimilation by the users more promptly than a mysterious electronic panel with light-emitting diodes.

Paradoxically, a lack of technical perfection, instead of being a hindrance, may constitute an advantage. A certain amount of dissatisfaction is necessary for proper development of an assimilation process. Criticizing techniques and developing intentions to think of better techniques are indications of interest.

This approach does not exclude the use of sophisticated methods. Reserve such methods for a subsequent phase, however, when manual items have demonstrated their value.

Visual media undergo dramatic changes. After several months of using a graph, it is not uncommon to implement another technique. Such evolution provides a reason not to develop techniques that are too costly or inflexible. Expect the constant remodeling of the visual landscape in keeping with changes affecting the plant, its methods, and its attitudes.

A Final Word of Advice

The selection of information and its mode of presentation, the physical preparation of media, and the selection of locations should be carried out in cooperation with the people employed in the production units.

The form of cooperation will vary in relation to the media, the company, and its management style, culture, and hierarchical structure. Keep in mind a fundamental principle: *An area's*

inhabitants are the first people to be concerned about visual organiza-
tion of their space.

TOMORROW'S FACTORIES

Having relied on sports images more than once, I will continue as I reach the conclusion. For a long time, production has
consisted of lifting dumb-bells. Each employee faces his or her
own cast-iron weight alone. A large amount of muscle is built,
so that many pounds can accumulate.

Today, different sports are involved. Now people are playing soccer – or basketball, handball, or water polo. Production
has become a team sport; we are involved in a competition –
either in the international leagues or on a less important level.

Recognizing the nature of the sport and the existence of
extremely well-organized competition, we must also acknowl-
edge that companies will never have winning plants if the chair-
person and a few executives are the only ones with a clear vision
of the game. Visibility must be expanded to strengthen the
group's cohesion. The time to light up the stadium has arrived.

I encountered this image of illuminated workplaces at the
Hewlett-Packard plant in Sunnyvale, California, where I was
welcomed by production manager Lee Rhodes. We sat in the
plant cafeteria, where the tables had been set out on a terrace.
California sunshine shimmered on the birches next to the main
building.

"In the United States," Rhodes explained, "many plants
still stubbornly practice a form of human resource management
that we call 'mushroom management.' Similar to the growing of
mushrooms, which need little light and much manure, mushroom management keeps workers in information darkness and
shovels on much hard work."

"Is it because there's so little to see?" Rhodes asked. "To
ignore the richness of information that is required in any production process and to further ignore the human potential for

processing that information is a holdover from the Dark Ages. It is no wonder that even with strong lighting, one has the impression of walking into darkness upon entering one of these production areas."

Visiting the visual workplaces described in this book, the opposite experience prevails: a feeling of being in a luminous place — clean, bright and colorful.

The factories of tomorrow will be enlightened factories.

About the Author

Michel Greif has taught Operations Management since 1980 at the Hautes Etudes Commerciales (HEC), Paris, the best-known business school in France. He worked from 1970 to 1980 as a vice president for manufacturing for Sevylor, a French producer of inflatable rafts. He has an engineering degree from L'Ecole Polytechnique, Paris, and a Ph.D. in geophysics. Dr. Greif is the author of *Gestion informatique de la production et des stocks* (Paris: Weka, 1984), and coauthor of *Management industriel et logistique* (Paris: Economica, 1990) and *Guide pratique du management* (Paris: Presses de la Cite, 1990).

Index

OTHER BOOKS ON MANUFACTURING IMPROVEMENT

Productivity Press publishes and distributes materials on continuous improvement in productivity, quality, customer service, and the creative involvement of all employees. Many of our products are direct source materials from Japan that have been translated into English for the first time and are available exclusively from Productivity. Supplemental products and services include newsletters, conferences, seminars, in-house training and consulting, audio-visual training programs, and industrial study missions. Call 1-800-274-9911 for our free book catalog.

The Battle to Stay Competitive:
Changing the Traditional Workplace
The Delco Moraine NDH Story
by Charles Birkholz and Jim Villella

This inspiring and quick-reading book tells the story of one company's nontraditional response to increased competition and threatened market share. It recalls in vivid detail the changes undertaken by Delco Moraine NDH, General Motor's Brake Systems Division, that earned them a position as a world class supplier of automotive components. This case study documents the company's efforts to strengthen their competitiveness through synchronous manufacturing=the coordination of resources (man, machine, and materials) to eliminate waste. The personal accounts of Charles Birkholz and Jim Villella, key players in the company's evolution, describe the various efforts at the floor level to change the standards and performance of their division of the decidedly traditional GM company.
ISBN 0-915299-96-8 / 208 pages / $9.95 / BATTLE-BK

20 Keys to Workplace Improvement
by Iwao Kobayashi

This easy-to-read introduction to the "20 keys" system presents an integrated approach to assessing and improving your company's competitive level. The book focuses on systematic improvement through five levels of achievement in such primary areas as industrial housekeeping, small group activities, quick changeover techniques, equipment maintenance, and computerization. A scoring guide is included, along with information to help plan a strategy for your company's world class improvement effort.
ISBN 0-915299-61-5 / 264 pages / $34.95 / Order code 20KEYS-BK

JIT Factory Revolution
A Pictorial Guide to Factory Design of the Future
by Hiroyuki Hirano / JIT Management Library

Here is the first-ever encyclopedic picture book of JIT. With 240 pages of photos, cartoons, and diagrams, this unprecedented behind-the-scenes look at actual production and assembly plants shows you exactly how JIT looks and functions. It shows you how to set up each area of a JIT plant and provides hundreds of useful ideas you can implement. If you've made the crucial decision to run production using JIT and want to show your employees what it's all about, this book is a must. The photographs, from Japanese production and assembly plants, provide vivid depictions of what work is like in a JIT environment. And the text, simple and easy to read, makes all the essentials crystal clear.
ISBN 0-915299-44-5 / 227 pages / $49.95 / Order code JITFAC-BK

Poka-Yoke
Improving Product Quality by Preventing Defects
compiled by Nikkan Kogyo Shimbun, Ltd./Factory Magazine (ed.) preface by Shigeo Shingo

If your goal is 100% zero defects, here is the book for you—a completely illustrated guide to poka-yoke (mistake-proofing) for supervisors and shop-floor workers. Many poka-yoke devices come from line workers and are implemented with the help of engineering staff. The result is better product quality—and greater participation by workers in efforts to improve your processes, your products, and your company as a whole.
ISBN 0-915299-31-3 / 288 pages / $59.95 / Order code IPOKA-BK

Kanban and Just-In-Time at Toyota
Management Begins at the Workplace (rev.)
Japan Management Association (ed.), David J. Lu (translator)

Based on seminars developed by Taiichi Ohno and others at Toyota for their major suppliers, this book is the best practical introduction to Just-In-Time available. Now in a newly expanded edition, it explains every aspect of a "pull" system in clear and simple terms — the underlying rationale, how to set up the system and get everyone involved, and how to refine it once it's in place. A groundbreaking and essential tool for companies beginning JIT implementation.
ISBN 0-915299-48-8 / 224 pages / $36.50 / Order code KAN-BK

Productivity Press, Inc., Dept. BK, P.O. Box 3007, Cambridge, MA 02140 1-800-274-9911

Total Manufacturing Management
Production Organization for the 1990s
by Giorgio Merli

One of Italy's leading consultants discusses the implementation of Just-In-Time and related methods (including QFD and TPM) in Western corporations. The author does not approach JIT from a mechanistic orientation aimed simply at production efficiency. Rather, he discusses JIT from the perspective of industrial strategy and as an overall organizational model. Here's a sophisticated program for organizational reform that shows how JIT can be applied even in types of production that have often been neglected in the West, including custom work.
ISBN 0-915299-58-5 / 224 pages / $39.95 / Order code TMM-BK

A Study of the Toyota Production System
From an Industrial Engineering Viewpoint (rev.)
by Shigeo Shingo

The "green book" that started it all — the first book in English on JIT, now completely revised and re-translated. Here is Dr. Shingo's classic industrial engineering rationale for the priority of process-based over operational improvements for manufacturing. He explains the basic mechanisms of the Toyota production system in a practical and simple way so that you can apply them in your own plant.
ISBN 0-915299-17-8 / 294 pages / Price $39.95 / Order code STREV-BK

New Production System
JIT Crossing Industry Boundaries
Isao Shinohara (ed.)

The most popular book on JIT in Japan today. Incorporating the ideas of Taiichi Ohno, it shows how the "New Production System," or NPS, works in a broad range of industries, including a garment factory, a fast food chain, and a lumber company. Differences in product are no excuse for the waste found in most manufacturing plants; see how to reevaluate business methods from the very root in order to achieve extremely efficient production.
ISBN 0-915299-21-6 / 224 pages / $34.95 / Order code NPS-BK

Productivity Press, Inc., Dept. BK, P.O. Box 3007, Cambridge, MA 02140 1-800-274-9911

COMPLETE LIST OF TITLES FROM PRODUCTIVITY PRESS

Akao, Yoji (ed.). **Quality Function Deployment: Integrating Customer Requirements into Product Design**
ISBN 0-915299-41-0 / 1990/ 387 pages / $ 75.00 / order code QFD

Asaka, Tetsuichi and Kazuo Ozeki (eds.). **Handbook of Quality Tools: The Japanese Approach**
ISBN 0-915299-45-3 / 1990 / 336 pages / $59.95 / order code HQT

Belohlav, James A. **Championship Management: An Action Model for High Performance**
ISBN 0-915299-76-3 / 1990 / 265 pages / $29.95 / order code CHAMPS

Christopher, William F. **Productivity Measurement Handbook**
ISBN 0-915299-05-4 / 1985 / 680 pages / $137.95 / order code PMH

D'Egidio, Franco. **The Service Era: Leadership in a Global Environment**
ISBN 0-915299-68-2 / 1990 / 165 pages / $29.95 / order code SERA

Ford, Henry. **Today and Tomorrow**
ISBN 0-915299-36-4 / 1988 / 286 pages / $24.95 / order code FORD

Fukuda, Ryuji. **CEDAC: A Tool for Continuous Systematic Improvement**
ISBN 0-915299-26-7 / 1990 / 144 pages / $49.95 / order code CEDAC

Fukuda, Ryuji. **Managerial Engineering: Techniques for Improving Quality and Productivity in the Workplace** (rev.)
ISBN 0-915299-09-7 / 1986 / 208 pages / $39.95 / order code ME

Hatakeyama, Yoshio. **Manager Revolution! A Guide to Survival in Today's Changing Workplace**
ISBN 0-915299-10-0 / 1986 / 208 pages / $24.95 / order code MREV

Hirano, Hiroyuki. **JIT Factory Revolution: A Pictorial Guide to Factory Design of the Future**
ISBN 0-915299-44-5 / 1989 / 227 pages / $49.95 / order code JITFAC

Hirano, Hiroyuki. **JIT Implementation Manual: The Complete Guide to Just-In-Time Manufacturing**
ISBN 0-915299-66-6 / 1990 / 1006 pages / $3500.00 / order code HIRANO

Horovitz, Jacques. **Winning Ways: Achieving Zero-Defect Service**
ISBN 0-915299-78-X / 1990 / 165 pages / $24.95 / order code WWAYS

Japan Human Relations Association (ed.). **The Idea Book: Improvement Through TEI (Total Employee Involvement)**
ISBN 0-915299-22-4 / 1988 / 232 pages / $49.95 / order code IDEA

Japan Human Relations Association (ed.). **The Service Industry Idea Book: Employee Involvement in Retail and Office Improvement**
ISBN 0-915299-65-8 / 1990 / 294 pages / $49.95 / order code SIDEA

Japan Management Association (ed.). **Kanban and Just-In-Time at Toyota: Management Begins at the Workplace** (Revised Ed.), Translated by David J. Lu
ISBN 0-915299-48-8 / 1989 / 224 pages / $36.50 / order code KAN

Japan Management Association and Constance E. Dyer. **The Canon Production System: Creative Involvement of the Total Workforce**
ISBN 0-915299-06-2 / 1987 / 251 pages / $36.95 / order code CAN

Jones, Karen (ed.). **The Best of TEI: Current Perspectives on Total Employee Involvement**
ISBN 0-915299-63-1 / 1989 / 502 pages / $175.00 / order code TEI

Productivity Press, Inc., Dept. BK, P.O. Box 3007, Cambridge, MA 02140 1-800-274-9911

Karatsu, Hajime. **Tough Words For American Industry**
ISBN 0-915299-25-9 / 1988 / 178 pages / $24.95 / order code TOUGH

Karatsu, Hajime. **TQC Wisdom of Japan: Managing for Total Quality Control**, Translated by David J. Lu
ISBN 0-915299-18-6 / 1988 / 136 pages / $34.95 / order code WISD

Kobayashi, Iwao. **20 Keys to Workplace Improvement**
ISBN 0-915299-61-5 / 1990 / 264 pages / $34.95 / order code 20KEYS

Lu, David J. **Inside Corporate Japan: The Art of Fumble-Free Management**
ISBN 0-915299-16-X / 1987 / 278 pages / $24.95 / order code ICJ

Merli, Giorgio. **Total Manufacturing Management: Production Organization for the 1990s**
ISBN 0-915299-58-5 / 1990 / 224 pages / $39.95 / order code TMM

Mizuno, Shigeru (ed.). **Management for Quality Improvement: The 7 New QC Tools**
ISBN 0-915299-29-1 / 1988 / 324 pages / $59.95 / order code 7QC

Monden, Yasuhiro and Michiharu Sakurai (eds.). **Japanese Management Accounting: A World Class Approach to Profit Management**
ISBN 0-915299-50-X / 1990 / 568 pages / $59.95 / order code JMACT

Nachi-Fujikoshi (ed.). **Training for TPM: A Manufacturing Success Story**
ISBN 0-915299-34-8 / 1990 / 320 pages / $59.95 / order code CTPM

Nakajima, Seiichi. **Introduction to TPM: Total Productive Maintenance**
ISBN 0-915299-23-2 / 1988 / 149 pages / $39.95 / order code ITPM

Nakajima, Seiichi. **TPM Development Program: Implementing Total Productive Maintenance**
ISBN 0-915299-37-2 / 1989 / 428 pages / $85.00 / order code DTPM

Nikkan Kogyo Shimbun, Ltd./Factory Magazine (ed.). **Poka-yoke: Improving Product Quality by Preventing Defects**
ISBN 0-915299-31-3 / 1989 / 288 pages / $59.95 / order code IPOKA

Ohno, Taiichi. **Toyota Production System: Beyond Large-Scale Production**
ISBN 0-915299-14-3 / 1988 / 162 pages / $39.95 / order code OTPS

Ohno, Taiichi. **Workplace Management**
ISBN 0-915299-19-4 / 1988 / 165 pages / $34.95 / order code WPM

Ohno, Taiichi and Setsuo Mito. **Just-In-Time for Today and Tomorrow**
ISBN 0-915299-20-8 / 1988 / 208 pages / $34.95 / order code OMJIT

Perigord, Michel. **Achieving Total Quality Management: A Program for Action**
ISBN 0-915299-60-7 / 1991 / 384 pages / $45.00 / order code ACHTQM

Psarouthakis, John. **Better Makes Us Best**
ISBN 0-915299-56-9 / 1989 / 112 pages / $16.95 / order code BMUB

Robson, Ross (ed.). **The Quality and Productivity Equation: American Corporate Strategies for the 1990s**
ISBN 0-915299-71-2 / 1990 / 558 pages / $29.95 / order code QPE

Shetty, Y.K and Vernon M. Buehler (eds.). **Competing Through Productivity and Quality**
ISBN 0-915299-43-7 / 1989 / 576 pages / $39.95 / order code COMP

Shingo, Shigeo. **Non-Stock Production: The Shingo System for Continuous Improvement**
ISBN 0-915299-30-5 / 1988 / 480 pages / $75.00 / order code NON

Productivity Press, Inc., Dept. BK, P.O. Box 3007, Cambridge, MA 02140 1-800-274-9911

Shingo, Shigeo. **A Revolution In Manufacturing: The SMED System**, Translated by Andrew P. Dillon
ISBN 0-915299-03-8 / 1985 / 383 pages / $70.00 / order code SMED

Shingo, Shigeo. **The Sayings of Shigeo Shingo: Key Strategies for Plant Improvement**, Translated by Andrew P. Dillon
ISBN 0-915299-15-1 / 1987 / 208 pages / $39.95 / order code SAY

Shingo, Shigeo. **A Study of the Toyota Production System from an Industrial Engineering Viewpoint** (rev.)
ISBN 0-915299-17-8 / 1989 / 293 pages / $39.95 / order code STREV

Shingo, Shigeo. **Zero Quality Control: Source Inspection and the Poka-yoke System**,Translated by Andrew P. Dillon
ISBN 0-915299-07-0 / 1986 / 328 pages / $70.00 / order code ZQC

Shinohara, Isao (ed.). **New Production System: JIT Crossing Industry Boundaries**
ISBN 0-915299-21-6 / 1988 / 224 pages / $34.95 / order code NPS

Sugiyama, Tomo. **The Improvement Book: Creating the Problem-Free Workplace**
ISBN 0-915299-47-X / 1989 / 236 pages / $49.95 / order code IB

Suzue, Toshio and Akira Kohdate. **Variety Reduction Program (VRP): A Production Strategy for Product Diversification**
ISBN 0-915299-32-1 / 1990 / 164 pages / $59.95 / order code VRP

Tateisi, Kazuma. **The Eternal Venture Spirit: An Executive's Practical Philosophy**
ISBN 0-915299-55-0 / 1989 / 208 pages/ $19.95 / order code EVS

Audio-Visual Programs

Japan Management Association. **Total Productive Maintenance: Maximizing Productivity and Quality**
ISBN 0-915299-46-1 / 167 slides / 1989 / $749.00 / order code STPM
ISBN 0-915299-49-6 / 2 videos / 1989 / $749.00 / order code VTPM

Shingo, Shigeo. **The SMED System**, Translated by Andrew P. Dillon
ISBN 0-915299-11-9 / 181 slides / 1986 / $749.00 / order code S5
ISBN 0-915299-27-5 / 2 videos / 1987 / $749.00 / order code V5

Shingo, Shigeo. The Poka-yoke System, Translated by Andrew P. Dillon
ISBN 0-915299-13-5 / 235 slides / 1987 / $749.00 / order code S6
ISBN 0-915299-28-3 / 2 videos / 1987 / $749.00 / order code V6

TO ORDER: Write, phone, or fax Productivity Press, Dept. BK, P.O. Box 3007, Cambridge, MA 02140, phone 1-800-274-9911, fax 617-864-6286. Send check or charge to your credit card (American Express, Visa, MasterCard accepted).

U.S. ORDERS: Add $4 shipping for first book, $2 each additional for UPS surface delivery. CT residents add 8% and MA residents 5% sales tax.

INTERNATIONAL ORDERS: Write, phone, or fax for quote and indicate shipping method desired. Pre-payment in U.S. dollars must accompany your order (checks must be drawn on U.S. banks). When quote is returned with payment, your order will be shipped promptly by the method requested.

NOTE: Prices subject to change without notice.